The Bicycle Rider's Bible

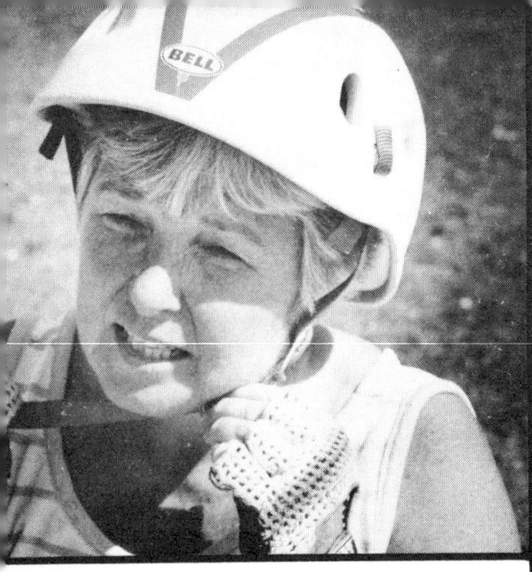
BELL

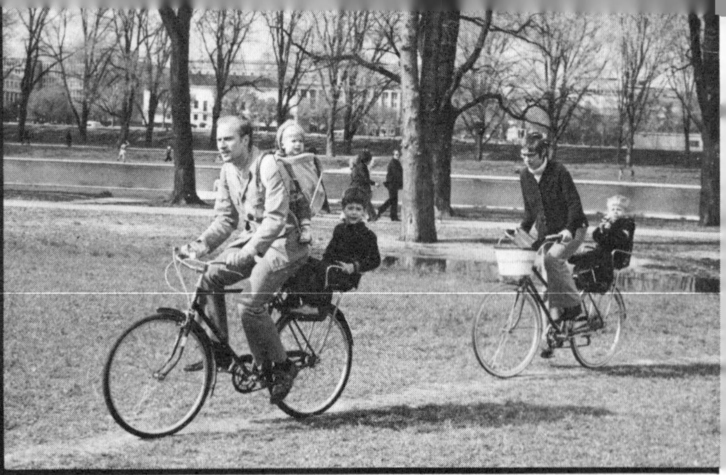

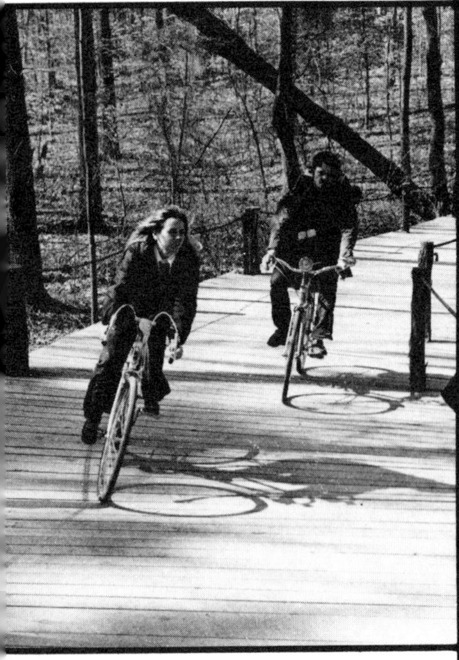

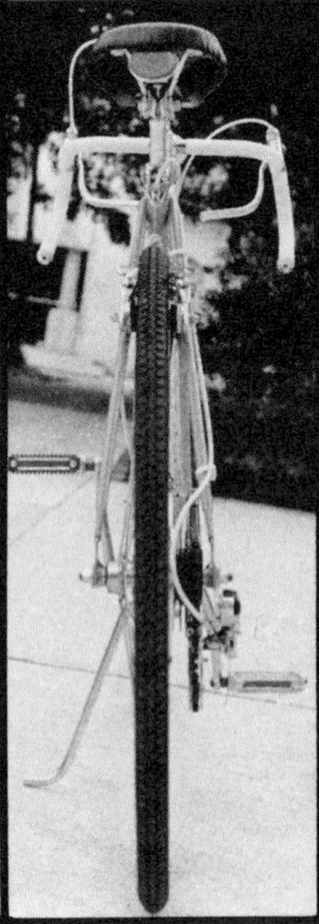

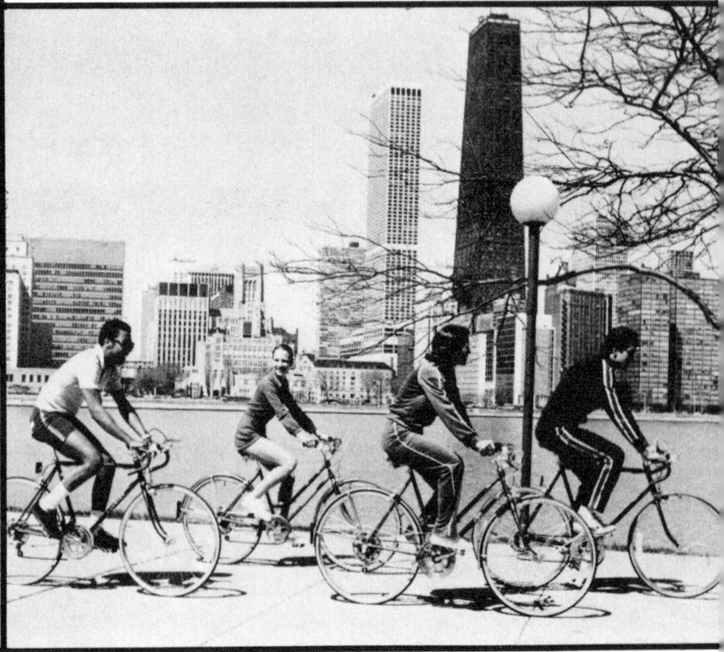

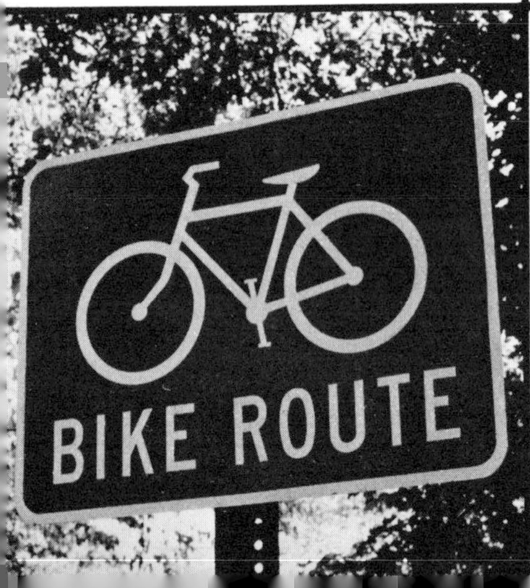
BIKE ROUTE

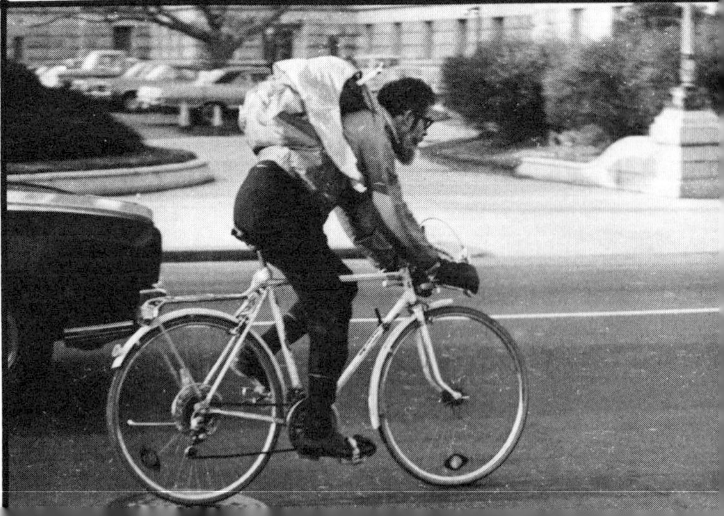

JEFF MARSHALL

The
Bicycle Rider's
Bible

Doubleday & Company, Inc.
Garden City, New York   1981

ISBN: 0-385-15134-9
Library of Congress Catalog Card Number 79-6868
Copyright © 1981 by Doubleday & Company, Inc.
All Rights Reserved
Printed in the United States of America

First Edition

BOOK DESIGN BY BENTE HAMANN

CONTENTS

CHAPTER		PAGE
1.	The Place of the Bicycle	1
2.	The Long Adventure	3
3.	Buying a Bicycle	8
4.	Know the Component Parts	35
5.	The Accessories	47
6.	Clothing	55
7.	Learning To Ride	58
8.	Transporting the Bicycle	64
9.	Those Big Rides	69
10.	The Bike Trails Are Waiting	73
11.	Bicycles in the National Parks	82
12.	The Touring Cyclist	94
13.	The Camping Cyclist	113
14.	The Racers	123
15.	The Bicycle Commuter	128
16.	Your Bicycle and Your Health	136
17.	Ride Safely	141
18.	The Bike Stealers	152
19.	Bicycle Maintenance	157

The Bicycle Rider's Bible

These bicycles provide transportation for students at the University of California, Davis. UNIVERSITY OF CALIFORNIA PHOTO.

1.
THE PLACE OF THE BICYCLE

Since the dawn of civilization people have dreamed of ways to travel with less effort and greater speed. We learned that we could climb onto the back of a horse and make it do the work. Then we found that by linking a couple of wheels together we could create a machine that would carry us under our own power. Next came the conversion of energy stored in coal, wood and oil to operate engines that moved trains, boats and finally, automobiles. These automobiles took over roads that had been dominated by horses and bicycles, and within a few years everyone wanted to ride in the newfangled vehicles and enjoy the luxury of letting fuel do the work. Bicycles, as might be expected, fell from popularity.

The bicycle, however, was not dead. Recently it has bounded back into the transportation picture and spurted far beyond any previous level of popularity. The estimated number of bicycles owned by Americans in 1960 stood at 23.5 million; approximately 20 years later the total had climbed to 90 million. The number of bicycles coming from factories across the country is greater than the annual production of automobiles.

There are several reasons why the bicycle is enjoying this new crest of popularity. Perhaps the most important is that bicycling is a sport that nearly anyone can participate in, no matter what his or her age might be. One eighty-year-old man joined the Bikecentennial riders of 1976, pedaling from coast to coast over a trail more than 4,000 miles long.

Meanwhile, entire families, equipped with bikes, can add a new dimension to their outings by sharing an exhilarating outdoor experience. Travelers speeding past them in gasoline-powered monsters really don't know what they miss —the smell of flowers and the new-mown hay, the sight of a red-tailed hawk hovering over a hillside and monarch butterflies fluttering along above the highway. Setting their own pace, bicyclists can explore quaint villages or sit for a while in the sunlight beside a stream.

Besides, the bicyclist does not need to stop at service stations for costly and increasingly rare fuel, a factor that will loom even larger as we enter an age of scarcity. Fuel costs have already helped bicycles dominate the roads in many European and Asian countries.

The bicycle is practical for short trips around the neighborhood—errands between home and the grocery store, library, school or shopping center. It is especially suitable for trips of less than five miles, and studies show that more than half of the trips made in automobiles fall into this range. If bicycles were used for these trips, the amount of fuel used for transportation would drop by 25 per cent. Estimates are that many families could save $1,000 a year.

These are major arguments in favor of the bicycle and its newfound role in modern society. There are others, including the improvement in physical condition that invariably results from bicycling. Most of all, however, bicycling gives the rider a sense of accomplishment. The bicycle gets the rider around by the use of his or her own muscles. There is satisfaction in knowing that you are independent and self-sufficient while others line up at gas pumps.

A bicycle, properly cared for, can last a lifetime. It can be adjusted to the rider and its parts can be replaced until the bike and rider fit together as a team. If the saddle is not comfortable, you may install another without a major investment. If you want to add or remove fenders, the task is quickly accomplished. If the handlebar or the seat needs adjusting, the problem can be corrected in minutes without going to a shop. Bicycling does not add to the burden of polluted air hanging so heavily above our cities, nor does the gentle whisper of your wheels increase the level of noise pollution.

Bicycles are especially common on college campuses. Because so many people ride bicycles at the University of California, Davis, some campus police had to change from automobiles to bicycles in order to get around and enforce traffic laws. In this community of 36,000 people there are an estimated 26,000 bicycles.

Bicycles have become far more than toys. It is true that most riders start young and that a large percentage of bicycles are ridden by young riders, but bicycling is reaching into the world of adults. One government study revealed that 56 per cent of Americans over twelve years old ride bicycles. This changing pattern came about in recent times as lightweight, multi-speed bicycles replaced the old-style, heavy bicycles. Adult models accounted for 20 per cent of sales in 1960 and 65 per cent in 1970. All of this points to an even brighter future for the bicycle.

2.

THE LONG ADVENTURE

On a cloudy June day, Kevin Aker rolled out of Reedsport, Oregon, on the start of his greatest adventure. He fitted his toes to the clips of his ten-speed, leaned forward, distributing his weight over the bicycle beneath him, and soon hit his normal pedaling cadence.

The trail on that first morning of Kevin's Bikecentennial ride led along a narrow road, up and down gentle slopes and beside the clear, rolling waters of the Smith River. There were eleven riders in the group strung out along the road. Their only hazards, at first, were occasional logging trucks coming down from the timbered hills with heavy Douglas fir.

Kevin's bicycle bore a somewhat heavier load than those of his companions. He carried a camera with extra lenses and a small tape recorder to capture his impressions of the trip. Packed into his panniers and handlebar bag were all the items he would need for several weeks on the road: extra clothing, sleeping bag, toilet articles, film, tools, parts for his bicycle. Taped to the rack over the back wheel were half a dozen spare spokes. Spare tubes for his clincher tires were beneath the saddle, and in one pack there was a short section of old tire in case he needed it to repair a blowout on the way.

"The first day," according to his record, "we only rode 37 miles to Benson Creek. The ride was along the river. We saw a small deer and a few chipmunks and squirrels. There were hawks, crows and other birds."

That night the group stopped at a little tent camp, put their bikes inside the tents and wearily spread their sleeping bags in an old cabin that protected them from the occasional rains filtering through the giant trees.

Meanwhile, other riders were also departing daily on cross-continent rides, some groups going east, other groups west, in the biggest such bicycle event ever. The idea had first come to Dan and Lys Burden, a bicycling couple from Missoula, Montana. They were looking ahead. The country's bicentennial celebration would be in 1976. To the Burdens there simply was no better way to celebrate this All-American event than to pedal across the continent and see America under their own power as only the bicyclist can. The idea sounded good to their friends and to other riders as well, and so was born the Bikecentennial. Their plan was for the organization to remain active even after the bicentennial celebration was over.

Plotting a bicycle trail across the entire United States is an overwhelming assignment. But the organizers had help. They also had a three-year start, because they began planning in 1973. Hundreds of bicyclists contributed information on roads and facilities along the way. Riders traveled the potential routes. Information flowed into the Montana headquarters. Gradually the route began to take shape on the map.

The Bikecentennial route was by no means the fastest way of riding from coast to coast. Instead,

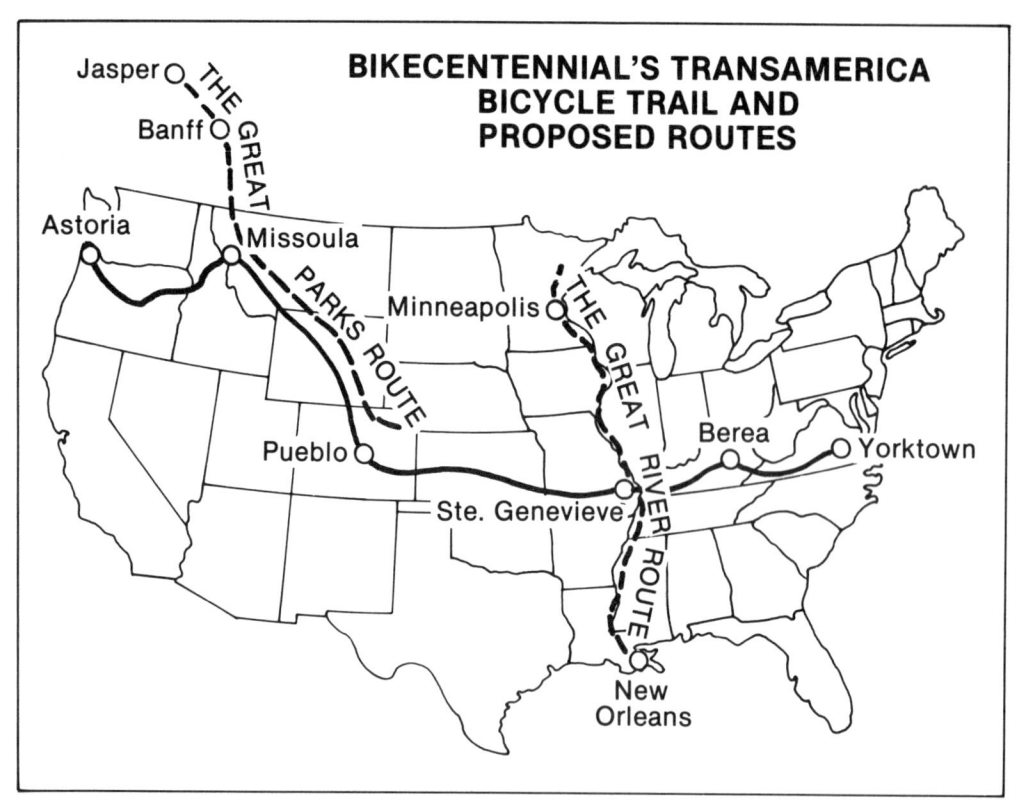

BIKECENTENNIAL'S TRANSAMERICA BICYCLE TRAIL AND PROPOSED ROUTES

COURTESY BIKECENTENNIAL.

it followed country roads, leading riders away from heavy traffic and into splendid national parks and scenic national forests. The route wandered through sleepy villages and gave a new look at how America lives and works. The total length of the trip from Astoria, Oregon, to Yorktown, Virginia, would be 4,250 miles through mountains, across plains and along river valleys.

All of the riders had given the coming trip much thought and planning. Kevin Aker had worked at trimming the weight of his equipment to a bare minimum. He had made practice runs out of Dayton, Ohio, to keep in shape, and had studied maps of the country through which the trail would lead. Finally, he had given his Huffy a final checkup and packed it with a high sense of excitement. Then he had headed west for the starting point—Reedsport, Oregon.

On the third day of the trip Kevin learned the advantages of being in good physical condition. The trail went along the scenic MacKenzie River for mile after mile. Kevin and his companions rode past tumbling white-water rapids and through spectacular mountain settings. Others had warned that this part of the ride would be difficult. "We heard stories about it," Kevin said, "and they all turned out to be true." The farther they pedaled into the mountains, the smaller the river became. Most of the time they pedaled in first gear. "We kept going up for four straight hours," Kevin recorded. The pass they might have taken was snowed in, and they had to turn to another that eventually led to a mountaintop elevation of 4,897 feet, through snowfields buffeted by bitter winds.

Before beginning the descent, Kevin put on the warmest clothes he carried and checked his bike to see that everything was working. Then, for fifteen minutes, it was downhill along a steep, twisting trail, an unforgettable ride. By now the riders were becoming conditioned for any challenge the trip might offer. And most of America still lay ahead of them.

High mountain passes continued to loom before them. Kevin was pleased with his equipment, especially the low gear on his bicycle. "A lot of people," he recorded, "are having to stand up on their bikes going up to the high passes. Because of my low first gearing, there is no problem for me. Just sit down and start pedaling." In western Montana, where the trail led from Darby to Wisdom, the group pedaled up and over Chief Joseph Pass, 7,241 feet, and Kevin considered it worth noting that, "Several cars were overheated along the trail and it was a real thrill to ride a bicycle right past them."

They encountered, for some days, members of another group, a fast-riding camping group covering from 100 to 150 miles a day and Kevin, whose longest day had been 84 miles, was grateful that their own schedule was not robbing them of the pleasure of seeing the country in good health. "They looked like warmed-over death," he said of the speeding riders, "and several of them had bad knees. They were really dead tired."

After Kevin's group toured Yellowstone National Park and pedaled on into the heart of Wyoming, they topped a pass near Lander and met the first Bikecentennial riders coming from the opposite direction. The plan was working. Other groups of cyclists were stretched out across the country in a two-way pattern.

In Colorado they topped a pass 11,600 feet above sea level. This climb was followed by a 13-mile downhill that made up for the long uphill grind. In the city of Pueblo, Colorado, the group realized that they had now covered 2,125 miles—half the distance of their cross-country ride. On a fine day in Kansas, Kevin rode 110 miles, his first century ride (100 miles in a 12-hour day), and another memorable point in his trip.

Their trail led through the Ozarks, on into Kentucky and the Appalachian Mountains, and eventually to Virginia. They crossed the finish line on August 29, after 81 days on the trail. "This was a fantastic experience," Kevin said. "I would not have missed it."

One of the riders who made the trip that summer was Richard Dougherty, a newspaper editor. "It's a hell of a country," he said after the first part of the ride was completed. "I wish everyone could do what we're doing. It would renew a lot of sagging spirits and perhaps dispel some of the doubts about the future of this country."

By the end of the summer of 1976, 4,065 people had ridden parts of the trail and 1,788 riders had completed the entire trip from coast to coast. But trips along the Bikecentennial trail have not ended. Each year other riders add their names to those who have seen America, coast to coast, by bicycle. For bicyclists everywhere this is the big ride.

Cross-country trips really began for bicyclists almost a century before that memorable summer of '76. But no one is likely to gain more fame for crossing the continent on a two-wheeler than Thomas Stevens. Tom made his trip in 1884 with one of those early high-wheeled bicycles. When he started from Oakland, California, Tom was twenty-nine and full of vinegar. A less determined rider might never have completed the trip, which was fraught with dangers that would turn most modern cyclists back. With the rider's weight almost above the front wheel, the constant problem was keeping the little back wheel on the ground. Turning was difficult and the slightest maneuver was often enough to pitch the rider into a ditch. A rider had to know how to fall, and it is said that the low number of tumbles taken was a measure of the success of a day's travel.

Finding his way by asking directions from town to town (maps might have helped, except for the fact that there were few roads to map), Tom finally made it to the Sacramento River, just as the stream was approaching full flood stage. The best way of getting to the other side seemed to be by pushing his bike across the railroad bridge. The bridge was a long one, but Tom paused and listened carefully, heard no hint of an approaching train, and hurried on, pushing his bike between the rails. He made it halfway before he sensed the distant rumble of an approaching train. There was no time to retreat, and no hope of going forward. His only escape was to get down under the bridge and perch on the undergirding. He wrestled his 50-pound bike into position under the bridge just as the train rumbled onto the approach. He held on tenaciously as the brawling river rolled along far beneath him and the freight train rumbled over the rails above his head.

After the river crossing Stevens decided to follow the railroad tracks wherever he could. There

Grandpa's bicycle perched its rider far above the ground. A good part of the rider's skill was in knowing how to take a fall. BICYCLE MANUFACTURERS ASSOCIATION OF AMERICA, INC., PHOTO.

were trails beside the railroad much of the way, and these were more passable than muddy farm roads. There were long stretches, however, of roadless, sandy desert where he had no alternative but to carry his bike.

Tom negotiated the Rocky Mountains and came down onto the plains. As far east as the Mississippi River the roads were still wretched, and whenever his high front wheel hung up in the mud, he went hurtling over the five-foot wheel to land on the trail again. Nonetheless, he made it to Chicago, then on into Ohio and Pennsylvania, where the roads were better. Bicycle clubs began joining him for short sections of the ride. Tom Stevens' journey ended after 103 days, in Boston, on August 4. Not content with his achievement, Stevens set off in 1885 on a bicycle trip around the world. That trip, which ended in 1887, made Stevens world famous for his prowess on the bicycle.

Modern bicyclists setting off on a cross-continent tour can look forward to fewer problems, better roads and more fun. This partially explains why a growing number have been making the trip in recent years.

If you dream of crossing America by bicycle, you can benefit by the experiences of those who have already made the trip, including the Bikecentennial riders. How long will it take to pedal from coast to coast? If you are a strong and determined rider you may average 100 miles a day and complete the trip in six weeks. This, however, will depend on a combination of factors, including weather, physical stamina and psychological conditioning. It will also depend on how much the rider wants to stop for visiting or sightseeing, how well his bicycle holds up under the stress, and whether or not the rider suffers accidents along the way. And there is, of course, the wind factor. Seasoned riders often choose to start a cross-country journey on the West Coast, even if they live in Maine. This puts the prevailing winds at the rider's back through most of the trip. The prevailing winds are generally from

Southwest to Northeast. Wind that pushes the rider forward is a blessing, as you will find out if you have to buck a 30-mile-an-hour headwind.

Transcontinental trips confront riders with a variety of hazards that they might not otherwise face in a lifetime of riding through the streets of their hometowns. There can be snowstorms in the Rockies in June and sandstorms on the plains; the heat of the desert is a constant presence and wild animals may be encountered along the way. A rider's positive and calm attitude becomes the best defense against unexpected troubles.

A tight schedule can create problems in itself, including a mental attitude that denies you the full measure of fun a long bicycle trip should offer. The cross-continent rider is better off allowing at least two months for the trip—ample time to stop and smell the flowers, slow down and admire the mountain vistas, and turn down inviting side roads to friendly country villages.

3.
BUYING A BICYCLE

When you go to purchase a bicycle for the first time, you walk into a jungle—row upon row of bicycles in a confusing array of colors and sizes confront you, and the longer you walk around looking at them, the more confused you may become. Therefore, you should narrow down your choices even before you head for the bicycle store.

First, choose between the one-speed, three-speed and ten-speed machines. If you are an adult buying for your own use, you will almost automatically rule out the one-speed coaster brake bikes. They are heavy and can take the knocks, but are not lightweight enough or versatile enough on the hills for most adults and are certainly not suited for long rides.

Next, you will consider the three-speeds, which are excellent for relatively level terrain and short trips. They are also just the thing for maneuvering through city traffic. But, because they lack the range of gears found in the ten-speeds, they have limitations in hilly country. If you are going to do much touring you should probably consider a ten-speed.

At this point, you are ready to survey the field and see what is available. You are going to find a wide variation in bicycle prices. The best general advice, if you are not extremely knowledgeable about bicycles, is to settle for one in the medium-price range and understand that you will have to ride it for a while before you fully appreciate its capabilities or its faults.

Some bicycles, especially high-quality ones, are sold fully assembled. Millions more are sold every year in their factory cartons, which the industry calls a "short pack." Let's examine the alternatives from the buyer's viewpoint.

If you want the bike to come to you ready to ride, no sweat and no skinned knuckles, deal with a store where bicycles are a major part of the business and where all bikes are sold ready for the road. A regular cyclery can generally offer full service when the bike needs repairs or adjustments.

On the other hand, department and discount stores usually do not service the bicycles they sell and might not even know how to put them together. The customer may be as knowledgeable about bicycles as the salesperson, perhaps more so. If the buyer wants it assembled, the store may provide this service for a fee (probably $10) and assign the job to a stock clerk.

The advantage of purchasing a bicycle in the carton is price. If the dollar difference justifies a home assembly job and you feel you can manage it, take your new bicycle home in a box. Complete instructions are packed in the carton.

One day, standing at the end of a production line in a major bicycle company's factory, I watched the inspectors pull a boxed bicycle off the line for checking. They opened the box, took out the parts and began assembling them. They checked to see that all parts and instructions were included. Then, when the bicycle was completed and the inspectors were satisfied, they began breaking the bike down and putting it back into the box the way they found it.

I was told that one of these inspectors could assemble a bike in twenty minutes. If hurried, he might shave a few minutes off that time. However, this is no indicator of how long it will take you or me to do the same job. Those inspectors assemble bicycles of the same kind every day—several hundred a year. If one of us sets out to do the same thing, we can expect to spend at least one and a half hours at the job, and probably a full evening.

When the boxed bicycle comes from the factory, generally the front wheel must be put on, as well as handlebars, pedals, and brake and gearshift levers. The saddle will probably have to be added. Then you must check and adjust the bike for the person who will ride it.

FITTING RIDER AND BICYCLE

I have often been in the neighborhood bicycle store and repair shop when a potential customer arrives to select a bicycle. The early steps in the process have already taken place. The customer has been to other stores and has compared prices, weights, frames, derailleurs, brakes, handlebars and saddles. The moment of truth is close, and the investigative process has narrowed down to fitting the chosen bicycle to the person who will ride it.

On the adult ten-speed bicycle, the frame may measure anywhere from 19 to 27 inches and must be selected with care if the machine is to fit the rider. If the frame is the proper size for you, you can straddle the bicycle's horizontal bar, while standing with your feet flat on the ground, and have an inch of clearance.

A ten-speed bicycle, properly adjusted to the rider, will not permit the feet to rest flat on the ground when the rider is seated. But by sliding forward off the saddle, the rider can drop his or her feet to the ground to keep the bicycle under control while stopping or starting.

If you are buying from an experienced dealer who wants his customers fitted to their bicycles as precisely as possible, he may suggest changes

A skilled factory worker builds bicycle wheels. BICYCLE MANUFACTURERS ASSOCIATION OF AMERICA, INC., PHOTO.

In a modern bicycle factory all parts are carefully inspected at every stage of production. BICYCLE MANUFACTURERS ASSOCIATION OF AMERICA, INC., PHOTO.

in handlebars and saddle. Either can be adjusted for the comfort of riders, whose body proportions vary. The saddle can be moved forward and backward, and it can be lowered or lifted. The handlebar stem should also be fitted to the rider's arm length. The distance from the back edge of the handlebars to the front of the saddle should equal the distance from fingertips to elbow. You can adjust the tilt of turned-down handlebars for the position that feels right to you. The longer you ride, the better you will understand the importance of proper handlebar adjustment.

CHILDREN'S BICYCLES

Bicycles manufactured for children come in a variety of sizes, styles and prices. The proliferating number of offbeat bicycles offered in recent years has not simplified the problem of matching the machine to the child. There are bicycles with high-rise handlebars, wheels of different sizes front and rear, a removable top tube for converting a boy's bicycle to a girl's model, other innovations that came as a result of the motocross idea, and more.

The question of size is basic. Children, like adults, must have bicycles that fit them if they are to enjoy riding and develop confidence. Regardless of age, the rider should be able to stand on the ground and have at least one inch of clearance between top tube and crotch. Measurements can be taken on a boy's model to tell what size to buy in a girl's bike. Buying a bicycle large and expecting the child to "grow into it" can be a serious mistake, because a bicycle too large for the rider—any rider—is dangerous. The rider cannot dismount easily, and this, aside from being a hazard in itself, affects confidence and control. As the child grows, the bicycle can be adjusted, within limits, by raising the handlebars and seat. At least 2½ inches of stem should remain within the tube for safety. The younger rider should not be given a machine that has caliper brakes or gear-shifting mechanisms. Instead, get the beginner a coaster brake model to ride until he or she is eight or nine years old. The coaster brake bicycle can usually take rougher treatment.

Another choice is the three-speed. Three-speed

A rugged bicycle that will hold up under rough knocks is ideal for younger riders. BICYCLE MANUFACTURERS ASSOCIATION OF AMERICA, INC., PHOTO.

bicycles are quite suitable for riders in the nine to twelve age bracket, but after that age, and probably before, the ten-speed becomes the one with the big appeal. Young riders demand ten-speed bikes for reasons that may be neither logical nor sound. They might do far better, in fact, on a bicycle that can take more of a beating. If the neighborhood is full of ten-speeds, however, the pressure is great.

My longtime personal opinion is that there are too many ten-speed bikes being sold in this country. Every kid on the block seems to demand a ten-speed, then try to ride it like a rodeo star. Why did they buy the ten-speeds when a three-speed with flat handlebars and a more comfortable saddle would have served them better? Mostly because the bicycle industry has nourished the idea that the ten-speed is the bike to have, and that anything else labels the rider as deprived or abnormal or both. The truth is that the three-speed would often be a better choice,

BUYING A BICYCLE

Woman's and Girl's Collegiate, coaster, single speed.
SCHWINN BICYCLE COMPANY.

Gran Tour 2. 27" lightweight ten-speed. ROSS BICYCLES.

for adults as well as younger riders. Most of the people who demand, and get, ten-speeds are not going to use all those gears. Nor are they going to take long tours where the ten-speed offers definite advantages. Many of these riders do not even have enough hills in their vicinity to make the ten-speed a sensible choice. We should not allow ourselves to be persuaded to buy anything but the bicycle that will give us the greatest pleasure and service, no matter what we are told by other riders or advertisements. The really unfortunate result of all those ten-speed bicycles being sold to people who don't need them is that the bicycles may end up sitting in the garage instead of being used. With this said, let's look at the factors involved in choosing a new ten-speed.

THE TEN-SPEED

When you set out cold to buy a new ten-speed bicycle, you will find that outwardly these bicycles may look much alike. You will probably be looking at models with 27-inch wheels carrying 1¼-inch clincher tires, dropped handlebars, narrow saddles and complicated-looking rear derailleurs to slide the chain from sprocket to sprocket. They will also have caliper brakes.

But there *are* differences among the models, and you begin to get the idea when you start checking price tags. You can find bicycles ranging from less than $100 to $500 or more. You should be prepared to spend at least $200 if you want to have a reliable bicycle that will continue

The three-speed bicycle is a good utility vehicle for short trips to shopping centers, tennis courts or the beach. BICYCLE MANUFACTURERS ASSOCIATION OF AMERICA, INC., PHOTO.

to please you as you become increasingly skilled and experienced.

One of the features for which you pay extra is lighter weight. You may find that one model, made of lighter alloys, is five pounds lighter than a cheaper model. Those pounds can be important on a ride that lasts all day. If you buy the lower-priced model, you will probably trade upward later. Extra money will also buy you quick-release wheels that can be taken off the bike in seconds without the use of tools. On higher-quality machines the parts are likely to last longer than those on lower-priced models and require less frequent adjustment. The adult rider looking for a first ten-speed usually does best to concentrate his search in the middle price range. Avoid the racing bicycles unless you plan to race. They are not well fitted to touring.

THREE-SPEED

One of my friends who has spent many years in the bicycle industry said, "Don't slight the three-speed in your book"—perhaps because too many bicyclists have done precisely this. The three-speed belongs somewhere between the old coaster brake bike and the modern ten-speed. It has some of the advantages of both, as it combines low-cost reliability with a choice of speeds that help take the strain out of modest hills. Besides, like the one-speed, it is far less likely to be stolen than a more costly bicycle.

The most important single question to ask yourself is what kind of riding you will do. If you will be riding mostly around town on trips of ten miles or less, where the hills are not especially steep, the three-speed may be all you need.

The three-speed is heavier than the good ten-speed, usually at least 25 per cent heavier. The tires are also bigger and require lower air pressures. This combination makes these bicycles somewhat harder to pedal than the lighter-weight ten-speeds.

The three-speed can be kept in good condition with less maintenance than the ten-speed. Some riders also argue that it is safer for congested city traffic because the rider sits upright, a position that is more comfortable for many riders, especially those with limited bicycling experience. (The saddle on three-speeds is also usually more comfortable than on ten-speeds.) This same upright position, however, will make the three-speed more tiring on the long tour.

The three-speed bicycle customarily has the simple lever-type shifting mechanism on the handlebars near the rider's hand. PHOTO BY THE AUTHOR.

Before buying a three-speed you should also ask yourself if your riding practices might change. Will you, after becoming accustomed to bicycle riding, want to add touring and bicycle vacationing to your local riding? If so, you will probably be better off to pass up the three-speed and go directly to the ten-speed, unless you are willing to own two bicycles.

RISE OF THE BMX

In the early 1970s, young riders in California began modifying their sturdy Schwinn Sting-ray bikes and turning them into machines for rough riding. Off came the banana seats, to be replaced by racing-style saddles. Other alterations followed. Fathers with motorcycling experience added their ideas on what would make these bicycles stronger and more maneuverable as the young riders rode across rough unpaved trails while practicing sliding turns and jumps. Those young riders did not realize it, but they were bringing to bicycling a new idea that would soon spread far beyond the borders of California.

The modifications continued. Handlebars were widened, then strengthened by adding a crossbar. Gradually the frames were standardized. Wheels were standardized at twenty inches. These new bicycles acquired their own special name. They were called "bicycle motocross" or, more commonly, BMX or MX.

What was really needed in the BMX was added strength so that the machine could absorb the rough treatment inflicted on it. Frames were reinforced to distribute stress. Seat posts became longer to adjust to the rider's size. Some of the wheels are spoked, but strong wheels made of metal or nylon have outpaced spoked wheels in popularity. Furthermore, the BMX machine is generally a single-speed bicycle equipped with coaster brakes.

The basic design runs through the whole BMX family, but modifications given them by their owners are endless, with bicycle shops always ready to replace standard parts with the rider's choice in everything from forks to crank.

A number of small shops in California devote themselves exclusively to modifying these bicycles; some have even become small-scale manufacturers. Major manufacturers, for their part,

The rugged BMX bikes are made to negotiate unpaved trails, but purchasers should remember that the low-cost bikes in this category may not be strong enough to stand up under rough treatment. SCHWINN BICYCLE COMPANY.

could not ignore the growing demand. They studied what the BMX riders wanted and added these machines to their lines. Within half a dozen years after the first such modifications were made, the BMX machines accounted for a large share of the total bicycle market. However, BMX riders often want a second bike for street use, or to ride to school.

The special materials and work built into the BMX is reflected in the price. The average rider out to buy a new BMX is likely to spend $150, although the price could go considerably higher. There are less expensive ones available, but these models at the low end of the price range are really not strong enough for the rough treatment given the BMX in sanctioned events. Though built to look like the BMX, these cheaper models are better suited for street use. The dealer can tell you whether the model you are considering is constructed to take the hard knocks of racing or stunt riding. Some carry labels warning riders against using them for rough rides. The temptation, however, to play rough rider with any bicycle that looks like a BMX may prove irresistible to young riders, and a stronger bike may prove to be the sound investment in the long run.

THE LADY'S BIKE

In the bicycle business, tradition dies slowly if at all, and one indicator is the fact that the standard women's bicycle without a top tube is still being sold, although in diminishing numbers. This frame style came to bicycling when women wore dresses that swept the ground. Their clothes were restrictive, and a bicycle with no top tube enabled female riders to mount a bike and pedal in spite of the clothing inflicted on them by Victorian traditions.

Watch the next group of tourists pedaling along the highway: chances are most of the women will be mounted on bicycles with top tubes. Why not? Cyclists, regardless of sex, dress much alike these days. The wonder is that these museum pieces did not fade from the scene sooner. The standard triangular frame gives the rider a stronger, lighter machine with shorter cable lengths needed for brakes and gears.

THE MIXTE

Some years ago manufacturers thought they had discovered the bicycle style suitable for everyone. The top tube was lowered at the back to a position halfway between the traditional men's and ladies' bicycle shapes. This design was called the "mixte" and some manufacturers geared up heavily to produce them. The mixte, however, proved to have one major disadvantage, at least from the manufacturer's viewpoint: people didn't buy enough of them. Once again tradition controlled the market. Mixte frames are still available and they are favored by some, especially as a lady's bike for neighborhood riding. They are an excellent choice for short people, who are not easily fitted with a standard top-tube frame.

CAM-OPERATED BICYCLES

A recent development, the Facet BioCam 50-Speed first appeared on the market in two models and a variety of sizes. This costly bicycle offers a power transmission system that does away with the standard chain drive. It is designed specifically for the distance cyclist and is said to make highly efficient use of the energy that goes into pedaling it. The manufacturer in fact claims a 10 per cent increase in efficiency over standard bicycles. For more information on the Facet BioCam contact Facet Cycle Works Inc., P.O. Box 50129, 2929 East Apache, Tulsa, Oklahoma 74150.

PORTABLE BICYCLES

In this age of miniaturization, inventors turned their attention to two-wheelers that could be folded into a small pack. There are numerous reasons why such a bicycle has appeal. Automobile tourists can put the folding bicycle inside the trunk instead of hanging it on an outside rack. Folded, the bicycle can be carried onto a bus or commuter train. It can be part of the regular equipment in a small plane, permitting the pilot

UO19C lightweight "mixte" frame. CYCLES PEUGEOT.

Bickerton folding bicycle. BICKERTON CYCLES, LTD.

to unfold his bicycle and ride away even from the smallest, most remote air strip. A commuter equipped with a folding bicycle can fold the machine, place it in its carrying bag and take it up to his office, eliminating worries about bicycle parking. It can be used on both ends of a commuter's train or bus trip. Boat owners also find these bicycles convenient.

All of these possibilities may have been in the mind of engineer Harry Bickerton, a British inventor, when he began building his first folding bicycle in the early 1970s. Bickerton's machine had small wheels and high handlebars, prompting some who first saw it to think it might have escaped from a clown act. But, on the plus side, it was a three-speed, easily folded and unfolded machine that provided a surprisingly smooth ride in view of its unorthodox design.

After a series of business arrangements over the following years, the Bickerton went into production and onto the market. Eventually, it showed up in a number of American outlets and on American streets. The folding bicycle was a product whose time had come, and interest in the Bickerton continues to grow.

These bicycles may never offer the smooth, energy-efficient ride of the ten-speed, but they do perform a wide range of jobs. Serious riders who buy a folding bicycle for commuting will also own a standard bicycle or two for touring and riding around home, but the portable bicycle complements those other bikes in the stable. If you want to investigate these folding machines,

A wide variety of tandem bicycles are available on today's market. Those who ride tandems should be of like temperament and have similar riding abilities. BICYCLE MANUFACTURERS ASSOCIATION OF AMERICA, INC., PHOTO.

get the name of your nearest dealer from either Handleman's, 16 Reservoir Road, White Plains, NY 10603, or Bickerton Cycles Ltd., 1314 N.W. Glisan Street, Portland, OR 97209.

As you begin shopping around for such a bicycle, you will discover that the Bickerton is only one of many mini-bikes being offered. The take-apart features on some models are a major attraction. So is the fact that seats and handlebars can be adjusted to fit riders of different sizes.

CHOOSING AND RIDING THE TANDEM

The bicycle built for two can be a pleasure or a disaster, and the couple contemplating purchase or long-distance riding of a tandem should talk with those who have tried it. Tandem bikes have a special appeal for some. Two riders pedaling along on their tandem can converse easily as they travel. They will probably make better time on one bike than on two.

On the other hand, the tandem is a demanding machine that requires teamwork. The person pedaling in the rear must be capable, both physically and mentally, of adapting to the riding style and the pedaling speed of the person in front. The front pedaler has to keep the other's abilities in mind, not pedal too fast, and give warnings before shifting gears, stopping or turning. The two must feel a certain satisfaction in the teamwork required to make a single machine do their joint bidding. Each rider has to pull his or her own weight. If one pedaler has to do most of the work, the tandem will never be highly satisfactory.

Tandems come in a variety of designs. You can choose one with standard men's-style frames both front and rear or one with a men's frame forward and a women's-style frame in the rear. You can also buy a tandem with different-size frames front and rear for different-size riders.

A good lightweight tandem is likely to weigh between 40 and 50 pounds, whereas a cheaper model may weigh twice as much. You should settle on a ten-speed or fifteen-speed lightweight tandem if you are at all serious about riding this style of bike and think you will want to use it for long tours and sight-seeing trips. The touring tandem should have standard-diameter high-pressure tires.

A tandem is more difficult to store and haul than the average bike. It is heavy and difficult to take up stairs. Parking can also be a problem. Remember, too, that the tandem is less maneuverable in traffic than a standard bike, but faster, especially on downhill runs.

CUSTOM-MADE BICYCLES

The last word in buying a bicycle is to order one made especially to your own measurements and needs. Custom-made bikes become objects of great pride for their owners. These individually fashioned bicycles, probably with Reynolds or Columbus tubing and Campagnolo quality components, set the owner apart in any group. But no bicycle should be bought for its snob appeal, and the lack of such a bike should never prevent the cyclist from enjoying his or her mass-produced model.

Too much is sometimes made of lightweight frames and bicycles fashioned in custom shops. For the average rider, the better answer is to settle for a mass-produced bicycle, not necessarily a ten-speed. Chances are excellent that, given a certain amount of care, the heavier bicycle is going to roll on through years of dependable service.

Custom-made machines do, however, have their place. If you decide on one, whether for racing, touring or ego satisfaction, you have numerous places to which you can turn. Recently there has been an increase in custom bike makers in this country. Or you can write to bike makers in Europe (including England, where there is the advantage of corresponding in a language understandable to both parties).

Cycling magazines carry information on custom frame builders. They may also be located by talking with others who have ordered custom frames.

THE USED BIKE

There are times when you can find an excellent buy in a used bike. But the pitfalls are many and a wise buyer is cautious. The more thoroughly you check the bicycle over, the better the chance for a good buy.

Used bicycles can be bought either from dealers or from private owners. (The latter can often be found through classified advertisements in newspapers.) Private owners may be willing to part with their bikes for lower prices than those quoted for similar bikes in the shops. On the other hand, a privately sold bike may have more undetected problems and unrepaired parts than bicycles that have gone through the dealer's shop. The dealer will spot problems in a used bike quickly. This does not always mean that he will have made the repairs needed, however, and for this reason the purchaser should make a thorough inspection of a used bicycle before buying, whether it is in a shop or the owner's garage. If you know what trouble signs to look for, you can usually tell in advance exactly what the bicycle will need to make it roadworthy.

Begin by going over the frame for signs of stress or evidence of wrecks. Check the areas where tubes join, searching for splits or rough sections. Even chipped paint can be a sign of trouble. If the bike has been wrecked, the frame may be out of line. The same rules that apply to choosing a new frame hold for the used one. The poorly constructed frame isn't going to improve with use.

Be certain that all the parts are there, and that no bolts are missing. If you are handy with tools, you may decide to buy the bike even if it does need adjustments and repairs, provided that the price makes the deal attractive.

Wheel condition is important. Turn the bike upside down and see how the wheels spin. If they are out of line and wobbly, you can soon detect this. A side-to-side wobbling may be due to a bent rim that needs replacing or to improperly adjusted spokes that can be corrected with a wheel truing job. Check the rim and hub carefully. Also look to see that all spokes are in place and in good condition. A wobbling wheel could also indicate that bearings are in poor condition or not properly adjusted. A rubbing wheel could mean that the forks are bent, especially if the problem cannot be eliminated by adjusting the wheel position.

While you have the bicycle upside down, you can also get a close look at the tires. Worn tires should, of course, be replaced, but remember that though a worn tire may mean only that the bike has been used, uneven wear may be an indication of an inproperly built or functioning wheel.

Also take a look at the chain. It can be an indicator of the care given to the bike by its previous owner. Bent or worn links, or rust on the chain, are clear signs that a replacement is called for. A damaged chain can cause excess wear on sprocket wheels and derailleur parts, and a close look will tell you if such damage has occurred. Even if the derailleur is bent and has to be replaced, the bike may be a sound investment if the asking price is low enough.

Smooth-shifting gears that stay in position are the least you should expect on a three-speed bike. If the gears are working poorly and adjustment does not clear up the problems, take the probable cost of repairs into account.

Pedals should work smoothly, hold firmly in position on threads that are not stripped and show no evidence of having been bent.

Riding the bicycle is a good way to see whether all the parts are working as they should. Are the brakes working and pulling evenly? Are gears doing the job they should? Do the wheels wobble? Will you enjoy riding this bike?

Wherever you are buying a used bike, time spent checking it out in advance is time well spent.

THE BICYCLE MARKET: A SELECTIVE SAMPLING

MODELS FOR CHILDREN AND YOUNG ADULTS

Lil' Tiger. SCHWINN BICYCLE COMPANY.

Lil' Chik. SCHWINN BICYCLE COMPANY.

Pixie Sting-ray. SCHWINN BICYCLE COMPANY.

Pixie II. SCHWINN BICYCLE COMPANY.

BUYING A BICYCLE 21

Boy's Collegiate, coaster.
SCHWINN BICYCLE COMPANY.

Girl's Varsity Sport ten-speed.
SCHWINN BICYCLE COMPANY.

Boy's Caliente ten-speed.
SCHWINN BICYCLE COMPANY.

SINGLE-SPEEDS

Man's Collegiate, coaster, single speed. SCHWINN BICYCLE COMPANY.

Dunerider, coaster, single speed. ROSS BICYCLES.

BUYING A BICYCLE

Heavy-duty woman's bicycle, 26″×2.125 balloon tires, wheels with 11g spokes. WORKSMAN CYCLES.

Heavy-duty man's bicycle, 26″×2.125 balloon tires, wheels with 11g spokes. WORKSMAN CYCLES.

Paramount Track Bike. SCHWINN BICYCLE COMPANY.

TEN-SPEEDS AND UP

Citation, 27″ men's ten-speed. MURRAY, OHIO, MANUFACTURING COMPANY.

Outrage. Men's 26″ twelve-speed. MURRAY, OHIO, MANUFACTURING COMPANY.

Santa Fe ten-speed bicycle in sizes 27″, 26″, 24″. HUFFY CORPORATION.

Bandit 20″. HUFFY CORPORATION.

Man's World Sport ten-speed. SCHWINN BICYCLE COMPANY.

Woman's World Sport ten-speed. SCHWINN BICYCLE COMPANY.

Man's Traveler III ten-speed. SCHWINN BICYCLE COMPANY.

Woman's Traveler III ten-speed. SCHWINN BICYCLE COMPANY.

BUYING A BICYCLE

Man's Varsity ten-speed.
SCHWINN BICYCLE COMPANY.

Man's Professional Road Racer Paramount. SCHWINN BICYCLE COMPANY.

Woman's Deluxe Touring Paramount, SCHWINN BICYCLE COMPANY.

Man's Deluxe Touring Paramount ten-speed. SCHWINN BICYCLE COMPANY.

Super Gran Tour 27". ROSS BICYCLES.

Gran Tour 27" bicycle, lightweight ten-speed. ROSS BICYCLES.

UO9 ten-speed touring bike.
CYCLES PEUGEOT.

UO10. CYCLES PEUGEOT.

UO8 lightweight ten-speed.
CYCLES PEUGEOT.

PX 10. CYCLES PEUGEOT.

THE BMX
AND OTHER VARIANTS

Team Murray BMX. MURRAY, OHIO, MANUFACTURING COMPANY.

Team Murray BMX. MURRAY, OHIO, MANUFACTURING COMPANY.

Charger-2T MX Bike. PANDA BIKE COMPANY.

Tornado. SCHWINN BICYCLE COMPANY.

Pro Thunder, motocross styled. HUFFY CORPORATION.

Snapper 20". ROSS BICYCLES.

Apollo 20" mag-style wheel. ROSS BICYCLES.

BUYING A BICYCLE

Mag Scrambler SX100.
SCHWINN BICYCLE COMPANY.

Competition Scrambler SX1000.
SCHWINN BICYCLE COMPANY.

Adult Tri-Wheeler. With three wheel brakes and both rear wheels powered equally. RET BAR CYCLE MANUFACTURING COMPANY, INC.

Deluxe Twinn Tandem five-speed. SCHWINN BICYCLE COMPANY.

Paramount Tandem. SCHWINN BICYCLE COMPANY.

4. KNOW THE COMPONENT PARTS

The basic element of any bicycle—the part that holds the machine together—is its frame. When you purchase a new bike, remember that frames, like apples, can be graded for quality. But first consider the frame parts.

The diamond frame is constructed of steel tubes welded or brazed together (see diagram). The seat tube, which extends from the saddle down to the crank hanger, is connected to the head tube, which holds the front fork and handlebars, by the top tube. The other major tube is the down tube, which connects the head tube with the crank hanger. In addition, a combination of seat stays and chain stays hold the rear wheel.

Most frames manufactured today, even on bicycles sold at modest prices, are going to go through life without breaking or bending. A rider should always realize, however, that the sections of a frame can and sometimes do come apart. Frames with cracks or obviously weak spots are a hazard. In such a case the bicycle should be checked by someone who can tell whether the Frames with cracks or obviously weak spots are placed.

Tubing used for making frames comes in two basic kinds, seamed or seamless. The tubing used on most bicycles of lower or average price is welded. It is rolled into tube shape from flat bands of steel that arrive at the factory in rolls. Heavy machines force it into tube shape and it is then welded automatically.

Seamless tubing is both lighter in weight and somewhat more responsive. Lesser rigidity means a softer ride, because proper flexibility enables the bicycle to absorb some of the road shock that in a more rigid frame is passed on to the rider. This is one reason the lightweight, more costly bicycles are expected to give the rider a less tiring ride on long trips.

Anything that can be done in the design of a bicycle to cut vibration saves energy. Engineers have found that much of the work done to pedal a bicycle can be drained off in vibration. This was especially important years ago when roads were rough, tires were solid rubber and movement seemed to be up and down as much as forward. One French engineer figured that one-sixth of a rider's energy was lost to vibration. In time, roads were improved and in 1888 pneumatic tires were invented. Later tires became smaller and higher in pressure. While the higher pressure and narrower width of tires reduced the drag caused by contact between tires and road surface, they did little to soften the ride. This made a springy frame all the more important. Some inventors attempted to equip bicycles with springs, but this never caught on, since it did increase weight. Serious touring cyclists today want high-quality, lightweight steel tubing that is strong without being heavy and rigid, but not so flexible that it absorbs significant energy.

Engineers are convinced that there is little that can be done to improve the basic diamond frame

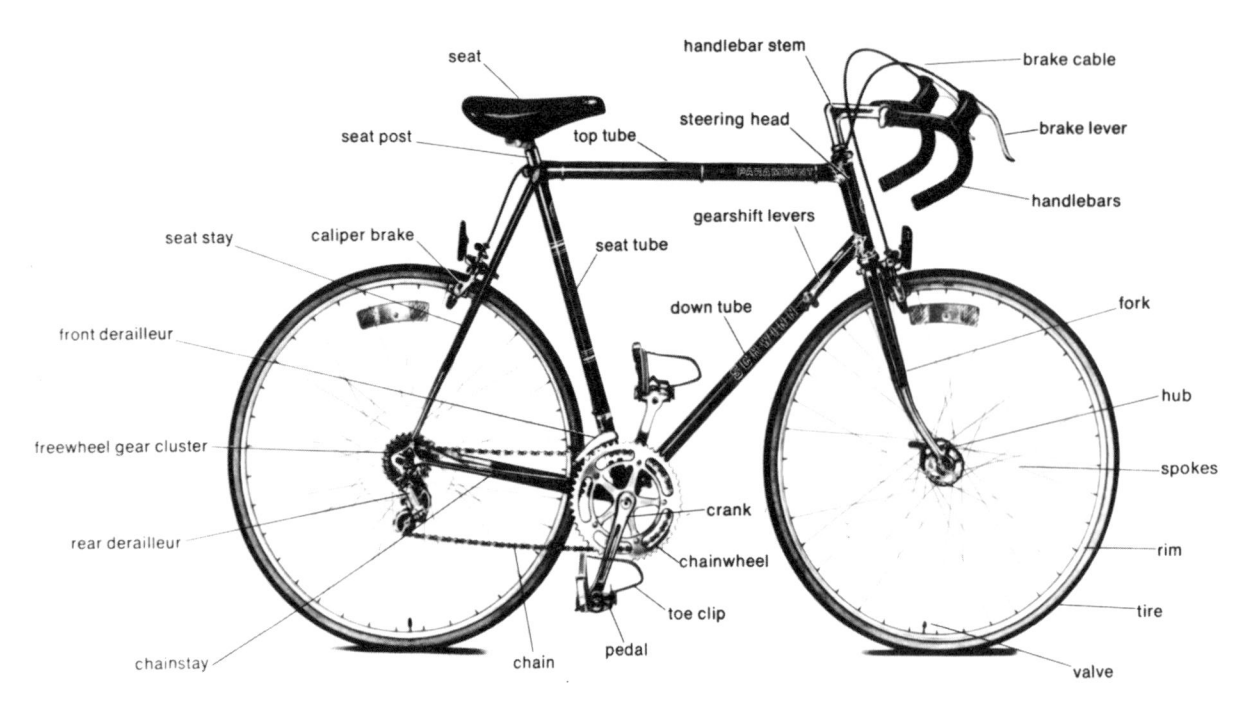

PARTS OF A BICYCLE

SCHWINN BICYCLE COMPANY.

Each frame is individually aligned in the factory. SCHWINN BICYCLE COMPANY.

Skilled workmen add the components to a finished frame. SCHWINN BICYCLE COMPANY.

bicycle design. The diamond shape gives efficient distribution of load, minimum structural weight and, combined with dropped handlebars, low wind resistance. There is frequent talk of using plastics for making lighter-weight frames, and this may someday be commonplace.

On many lower-priced bicycles, the frame tubes are attached to each other by simply welding them in place. The steel tubing on these bikes is of uniform thickness for the full length of each tube.

Higher-priced bicycles, however, are made of double-butted tubing, which is thicker at the ends where the parts of the frame will be attached to each other. This imparts added strength. In addition, the high-quality bicycle may have lugged frames with mitered tubing. This means the ends of the frame's tubes butt against each other precisely inside lugs which are generally brazed there instead of being welded. Because brazing requires less heat than welding, it is less likely to weaken the tubing. When you purchase a high-quality bicycle, the salesperson will probably point out that the frame is lugged or the tubing is double-butted. You can see the lugging for yourself.

Some bicyclists insist on frames made of high-quality steels, such as the famous Reynolds "531" or the Columbus. These are European products. You can tell if a frame is made with Reynolds "531" because there is usually a special decal attached, identifying the tubing. These special steels are most important to the purist who intends to use his bicycle for racing or extensive touring. The average cyclist is not going to worry too much about them. But anyone intending to ride on long tours should keep in mind the comparative weights of different frame materials and the ability of some more flexible frames to cut down fatigue.

WHEELS

The average bicycle buyer does not give much thought to the wheels, at least at first. They are there, front and rear, and as long as they revolve and are reasonably true, it is assumed that they are going to do their job. If you understand the nature of the bicycle wheel, however, you are more likely to treat it well and you'll have a bicycle that works smoothly for much longer than the one that takes a lot of knocking around.

The wheel, composed basically of hub, spokes and rim, is a precision part of the bicycle. Unless all the parts are in good shape, properly fitted and adjusted, the wheel is not going to serve you well. Tightening spokes applies tension; when properly spoked and adjusted, the rim is perfectly round and true. When spun, it does not move sideways. A loose spoke or two can distort the wheel's shape, giving a bumpier ride and causing excess and uneven tire wear.

Higher-priced bicycles are equipped with quick-release wheels. Instead of removing these wheels by first loosening or removing nuts on the ends of the axles, one releases the wheels by turning levers; this allows you to take a wheel from your bicycle anywhere in a matter of seconds, without tools.

If you could visit a bicycle factory, you might come away with a better understanding of what goes into the making of a modern bicycle wheel. In the big mass-production bicycle plants, coiled stainless steel wire is cut and shaped into spokes while bands of flat steel are fed from reels into powerful machines that shape it by stages into rims.

Meanwhile, hubs are traveling on another production line. All of the components merge on assembly lines where skilled workers lace the rims with spokes. The wheels go into a machine that places and tightens nipples on each spoke. They are then inspected to ensure that every part is properly in place and that the completed wheel is true.

Bicycle wheels normally have 36 steel spokes. The exceptions are found on smaller bicycles for children and on some racing bikes whose riders seek to reduce weight to the absolute minimum (in the latter case special hubs and rims allow for a reduction in the number of spokes).

TIRES

The bicycle tire is a sophisticated element of the bicycle. Any modern bicycle rider will have difficulty imagining what it was like to ride a bike with solid rubber tires, but early riders knew no other kind. Heavy, unresponsive and bumpy, in other words, a slow ride. That is, until a rider in Belfast, Ireland, tackled the problem.

John Dunlop was handy with tools, but not really an inventor. He was a successful veterinarian who, in his spare time, fashioned toys and other useful objects for his family. If a family member had a complaint that seemed legitimate, Dr. Dunlop would try to solve the problem. One day his son, Johnny, told the doctor that his tricycle was a hard ride any way you pedaled it. Working in a spare bedroom, Dunlop began making what he thought might be a better tire. He first went to the local store and purchased some 1/32-inch-thick sheet rubber. He cut this and shaped it into an airtight tube.

Next, he began cutting strips of linen from one of his wife's old dresses. These he wrapped around the tube, which he then filled with air. The time had now come for the first test. He took a wheel equipped with the air-filled tire and a similar one with a solid rubber tire out into his barnyard. He began rolling them side by side. The solid tire came to a stop quickly, but the air-filled tire continued to roll on until it bumped into the barn.

Dr. Dunlop then equipped his son's tricycle with the new tires, which his son agreed were a distinct improvement.

Dunlop, his immediate problem solved, could have stopped at this point. Instead, he bought a bicycle and a set of wheels for it made to his specifications. These wheels had rims fashioned to receive inflated tires. After bicycles equipped with his tires began winning races there was an immediate demand for pneumatic tires. The new tires were ready and waiting for the earliest automobile and the first airplane, as well as for the millions of bicycles built since.

The small-diameter, high-pressure tires used on lightweight bicycles come in two types. One is the tubular tire, about which the average rider will probably never worry much. These tires are used primarily by racers and by touring bicyclists who have become very serious and demanding about their equipment. The tubular tire weighs less than the more common tires and can be made to carry higher pressures that minimize rolling resistance. They are easy to roll up and carry as spares, and tourists traveling over long distances with this kind of tire normally carry several extras. They are delicate and highly susceptible to puncture from foreign materials on the road. The tubes are so thin that they lose air noticeably overnight. If you travel on tubulars, you must check at every opportunity to see that air pressure is up to the recommended level.

These tires are stitched along the inside, which makes repairing one of them a time-consuming task. They are seated to the rims with a light, even coating of rim adhesive; between the tire and the rim is a rim strip, which protects the tire from spoke nipples and gives the tire a smoother surface and less chance of puncture from the inside.

Only the lightweight racing bicycles come equipped with tubulars or "sew-ups." Far more common are "wired on" or clincher tires, which are made stronger by thin wires embedded in the bead of the tire where it connects with the upper edge of the rim. The heavier clinchers take the knocks better than tubulars on the road. Besides, they are easier to repair than tubulars.

The choice is actually much broader than this survey makes it appear. Within the two major types of tires available there are numerous designs and a variety of treads made for special road conditions and needs.

BRAKES

Every bicycle should have a braking system that is responsive and positive and that enables the rider to stop smoothly and quickly. A rider should understand the basic principles that make the brakes on the bicycle work. Then he or she can make minor adjustments to keep the brakes in perfect working order, or at least can recognize the problem that needs correcting.

There are two basic types of brakes in wide usage: coaster brakes and hand-operated cable-pull or caliper brakes. Some of us grew up on heavy-tired, one-speed jobs equipped with coaster brakes encased in the rear hub. Coaster brakes are activated by turning the pedals backward; the harder the rider pushes backward, the tighter the brakes set. The bike equipped with coaster brakes can be slowed gradually, or it can be put into a locked-wheel skid which invites disaster, especially where there is dirt or water on the road surface.

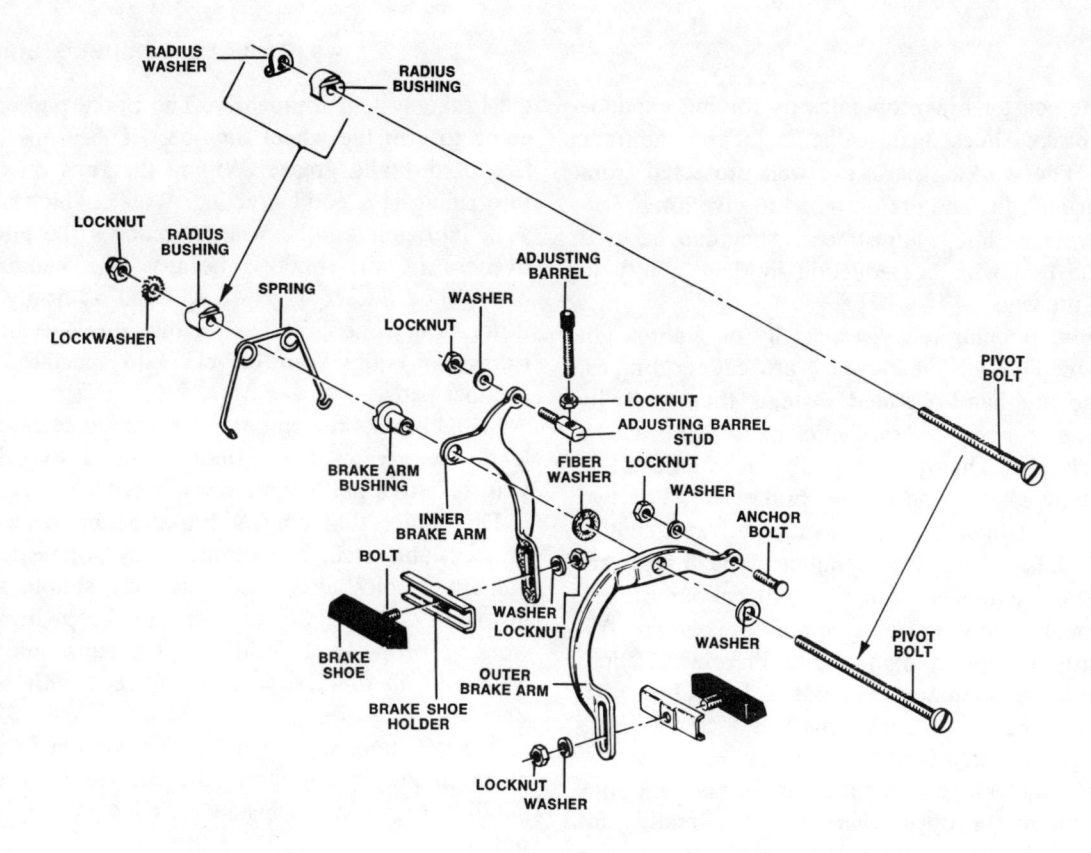

Exploded view of Philips side-pull caliper brake. SCHWINN BICYCLE COMPANY.

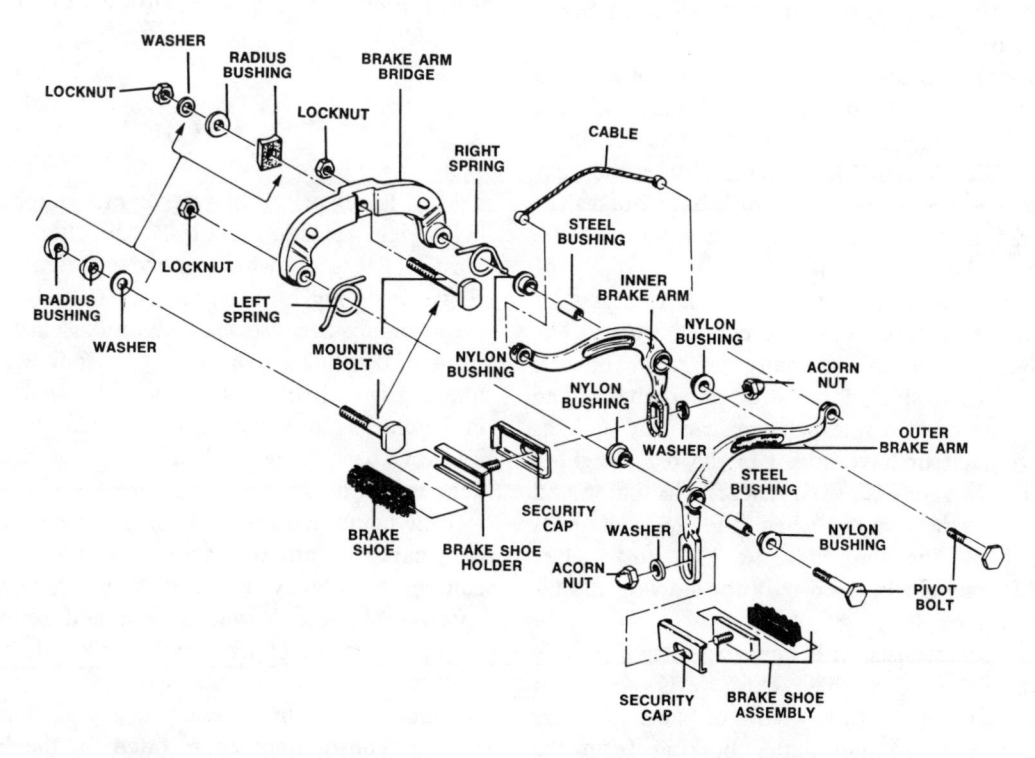

Exploded view of Weinmann Vainqueur 999 center-pull caliper brake. SCHWINN BICYCLE COMPANY.

The coaster brake operates by forcing expanding brake shoes against the inside of the rear hub. The working parts are well protected from water and dirt and are designed to give long service with minimum adjustment. They can be used in the rain with no reduction in their ability to stop the wheel.

More popular today, especially on lightweight and medium-weight bicycles, are caliper brakes. These are hand-operated systems that work by forcing rubber or synthetic pads against the wheel rims. They are generally more efficient in stopping a bike than coaster brakes are. The two types of caliper brakes are side-pull and center-pull. Less expensive derailleur-type bikes are generally equipped with side-pull caliper brakes, although well-designed side-pull brakes are frequently found on high-quality bicycles. Caliper brakes are commonly operated by cables that connect the brake handle controls with the braking mechanism mounted on the frame.

One advantage of caliper brakes is that they are out in the open where they are readily inspected. These brakes provide a highly effective way to stop a bicycle, although their efficiency in wet weather may vary with the quality of brake pad used.

Ten-speed bikes are normally equipped with caliper brakes on both front and back wheels. The front brake is activated with the left-hand lever while the right-hand lever works the rear brake. The safest plan is to work both brakes together, but if only one is used it should be the brake on the back wheel.

Some bicycles are equipped with two sets of hand levers for operating the caliper brakes. The standard levers are normally mounted on the front of each side of the drop handlebars. The second set of levers, which you can buy and install yourself or have added in the bicycle shop, are called "safety" levers. These ride flatter and closer to the hands when the handlebar is gripped on the top, close to the post. They should generally be used only for slowing the bicycle, not for stopping.

Serious bicyclists with long experience usually prefer not to have these extra levers on their bikes, claiming that they can be sure of more positive response and better braking from the standard levers.

Bike owners with caliper brakes should inspect the brake system frequently. The brake pads are going to grip the wheel rims best if the rims are free of dirt and grease. Wiping the rims off before riding is a good practice. Water, which acts as a lubricant on the wheels, reduces the effectiveness of the brakes, because the standard brake shoe does not grip a wet rim as firmly as it does a dry one. So allow for this in wet-weather riding, or equip your bicycle with special wet-weather pads.

In addition, remember that the heavier the load, the greater the distance needed to bring your bike to a halt from a given speed.

The cables that control brake action need to be well-lubricated, or else they may not respond quickly. Cables also need relatively simple adjustments from time to time to keep brakes working properly. In addition, the pads tend to wear and, in time, should be replaced with new ones.

A less commonly used braking system is the drum brake, which stops the bicycle with expanding brake shoes inside a casing at the rear hub.

Disk brakes, which are attached to the rear wheel only, are cable-controlled and hand-operated.

SADDLES

Most lower-priced bicycles come equipped with lightweight plastic saddles. An alternative to plastic is leather, which many experienced bicyclists, including both racers and tourists, recommend highly because leather, unlike plastic, will, in time, take on the shape of your individual contours, just as leather shoes do. The well-broken-in leather saddle becomes a prized possession. Treating it with neat's-foot oil or mink oil will help soften it and speed the breaking-in process. Recent manufacturing advances have brought to the market synthetic saddle materials that are gaining popularity because they are relatively comfortable, are lower in cost and require no break-in period. Unlike leather, they do not absorb water.

Saddles come in a variety of styles, depending on the type of handlebars fitted on the bike. If your bike has conventional "upright" handlebars, the rider's weight goes primarily on the saddle

KNOW THE COMPONENT PARTS

Continental-style saddle with foam padding. TROXEL MANUFACTURING COMPANY.

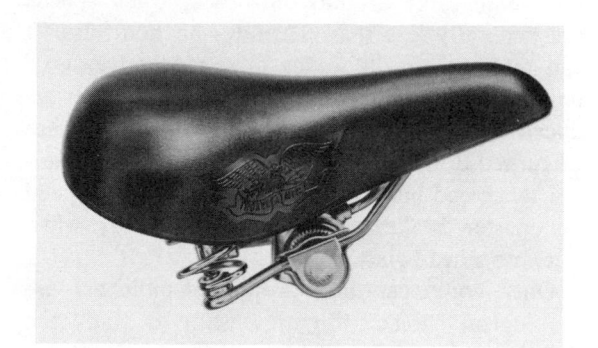

Deluxe model racing saddle. TROXEL MANUFACTURING COMPANY.

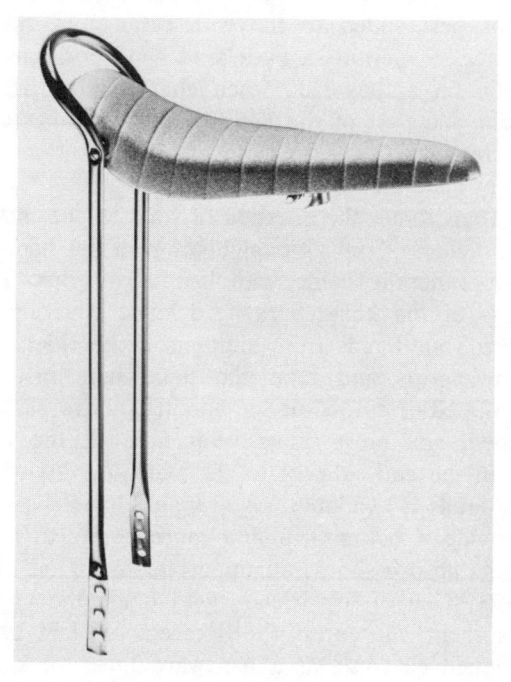

Banana seat. Vinyl. TROXEL MANUFACTURING COMPANY.

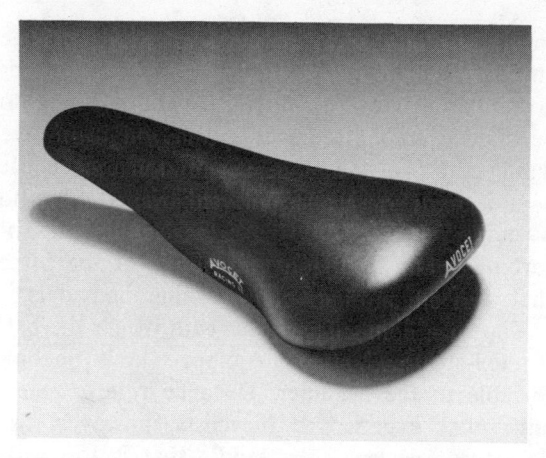

Lightweight racing-model saddle. Nylon shell and firm padding. AVOCET, INC.

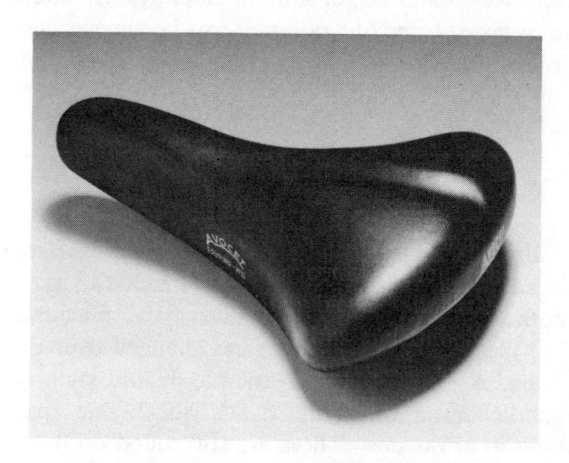

Woman's touring saddle. AVOCET, INC.

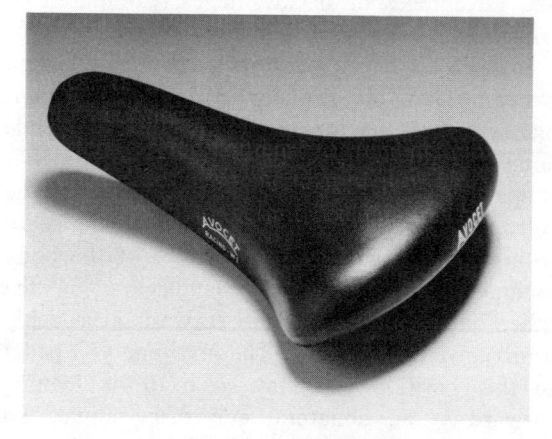

Woman's racing saddle. AVOCET, INC.

and the softer, springy saddle is likely to be the choice. On the other hand, if the bike has turned-down handlebars, the rider's weight is going to be divided among the saddle, the pedals and the handlebars. In this case a large, wide saddle would eventually prove both uncomfortable and wasteful of energy. A saddle with a shock-absorbing spring in it drains off some of the force that would otherwise go into pushing the pedals.

Those little narrow saddles with which the better ten-speed bikes are equipped look uncomfortable to the beginner. Distance riders, racers and other experienced bicyclists, however, use only these designs. The saddle that is too wide can rub the legs and make them sore.

Saddles come in a wide variety and the choice is a matter of individual preference. The bicyclist who feels the need for a more comfortable saddle may instead need to ride more to become accustomed to a narrow saddle that gives maximum efficiency in the use of energy.

HANDLEBARS

From its inception the bicycle has possessed handlebars or hand grips, with which the rider both balances himself and steers the machine, but the shape of handlebars has changed over the years. As a youngster, I knew only the style of handlebar on which the hands ride higher than the top of the post. These are still found on practically all lower-priced bicycles with coaster brakes, as well as on most three-speed bikes. We never thought about whether these handlebars had advantages or disadvantages. Compared to what? They were all we had and they did the job.

Instead of these older-style flat handlebars, many modern bicycles now have dropped handlebars which are turned down so that the ends come below the top of the post. This handlebar shape has a profound effect on the position of the rider. With flat "upright" handlebars, you pedal sitting upright, with the full surface of the body facing the wind; dropped handlebars, on the other hand, make you lean forward at roughly a forty-five degree angle. The first time you pedal in this position you may seem to be leaning forward at an unnatural and tiring angle. To experienced racers and tourists, however, there is simply no question about the superiority of the dropped handlebars for comfort and efficient use of energy, especially on long rides. This position also permits the rider to breathe more easily than when riding upright.

Using dropped handlebars allows the rider to distribute weight between the saddle and the handlebars. The combination of a high, small saddle and dropped handlebars enables the rider to transfer energy from his body to the pedals with maximum efficiency, because he can extend his leg farther.

Wind resistance may not be a serious factor in riding to and from the corner store, or in taking an evening ride around the block, when speeds are generally less than 10 miles an hour. But it can make a big difference in speed and ease of pedaling for the touring rider or racer. The reduced wind resistance experienced with the use of turned-down handlebars helps make the modern ten-speed bike far superior to the three-speed or coaster brake bike for long trips or when bucking a headwind.

Once convinced that dropped handlebars are the logical choice, you may want to study the different shapes available. These designs are named for noted riders who first used and popularized them. Among the best-known are the Maes, Pista and Randonneur. The latter is perhaps best suited to the widest range of riders because it permits a variety of hand positions, a boon on a long ride when changing the hands from one part of the handlebars to another can be restful. If you are going to race, you should investigate the Pista handlebars.

Then comes the question of what to put on the handlebars. Conventional bikes with flat handlebars generally come with handlebar grips. The ends of the handlebars need some covering to keep your hands from slipping. Some riders remove grips and tape the handlebars instead. Dropped or turned-under handlebars are usually taped, and most riders want tape all the way from the ends almost to the stem. A variety of materials is available for wrapping handlebars to provide a better grip and more comfort. Tape helps absorb shock, an important factor on long rides. One of my friends who made the cross-continent ride during the Bikecentennial in 1976 stopped en route at a hardware store for some new taping material. He wrapped his handlebars with the foam-type material used to insulate water pipes and later declared it excellent for softening the shock against his tingling hands.

When I wrap a pair of handlebars, I start about two inches from the extension that holds the handlebars to the post. Spiral the tape evenly around the handlebar, taking care to cover all of the metal neatly. At the end of the handlebar, stuff some tape into the hollow end of the tube. Then close the tube with a plug available from your bike shop. Do the same on the other side.

I have hesitated to mention here the handlebars some kids like because they resemble motorcycle equipment. These high-rise handlebars keep the rider's hands above chin level and have few redeeming virtues. They give a rider poor control over his bike and for this reason can increase the potential for accidents.

PEDALS

There are two major designs in pedals. One is the American style, equipped with blocks of hard rubber on which the feet ride. Most of us start out pushing pedals of this design, because they normally come on bicycles made for children.

However, when you graduate to a more expensive derailleur-equipped bicycle, you are going to use pedals made without rubber blocks. These pedals are all metal, with outside edges usually toothed in various patterns to give a more positive grip on the shoe. These are known as "rat-trap" pedals, or continental pedals.

In either kind of pedal there is a wide variety of designs, although the basic working parts are essentially the same. Rattrap pedals have a cap on the outer end of the spindle, and if you remove this dust cap, you can get to the working parts inside the pedal for cleaning, lubricating and repairing. The American-style pedals, on the other hand, have to be removed from the crank to be cleaned or lubricated.

TOE CLIPS

Some riders pedal without toe clips; others insist on them. The decision is a personal one and the individual has to look at his own bicycle and riding habits and weigh the advantages and disadvantages.

A toe clip is a metal bracket fitted to the front of the pedal so it curves up over the toe of the rider's shoe. It is normally supplemented with an adjustable strap that holds the toe firmly in position on the pedal. Toe clips used to be installed only on lightweight bicycles and on rattrap pedals, but now also appear on many heavier ten-speed machines. Beginning riders should not try to use them until they have mastered riding and developed skill in handling their bicycles. Toe clips are easily removed and re-installed later.

The big advantage of toe clips on the pedals is that the rider can get an extra boost from the energy expended. The foot fitted into a clip not only exerts pressure on the downstroke, but also can develop power on the upstroke by lifting the toe against the clip. On long tours, or when racing, the toe clip is essential.

The major disadvantage is that toes stuck into clips are not as easily or quickly disengaged from pedals. This scares off some riders. One in-between solution is to equip the bike with strapless clips. Then, in case of need, you can easily slip the toe out of the clip. Another possibility is simply to keep the straps adjusted loosely. To get a foot on the ground easily in heavy traffic some riders keep one foot out of the clip by using the other side of the pedal.

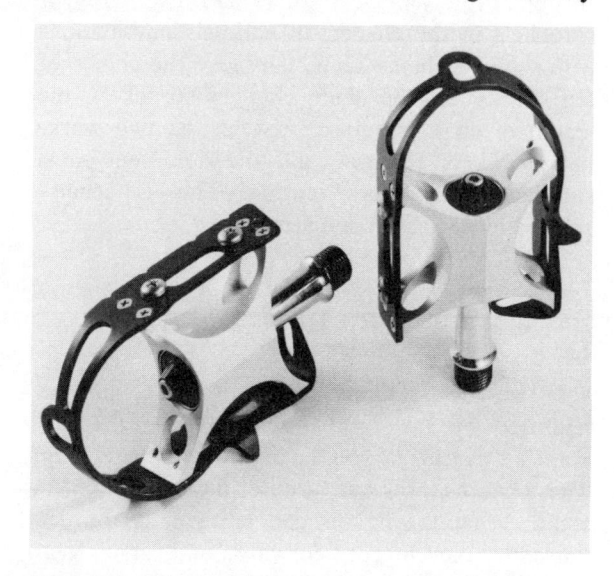

Ultra-light professional ten-speed pedals with titanium spindle. Weight: track 8.25 oz., road 8.75 oz. DEMCO BICYCLE PRODUCTS DIVISION.

Learning to use toe clips may take a little time and practice. Without clips the pedal has no top or bottom. Both sides are identical. But with clips attached, you must learn to turn the pedal up so the clip receives the toe of your shoe.

DERAILLEURS

Few more important developments have occurred in the history of the bicycle than the invention of the derailleur system, which permits riders to shift gears. The advantages are obvious, especially if you ride frequently on trails that take you up and down hill. When a gear-shifting system is working properly, an experienced rider's legs do not slow down even on the hard uphill pulls. The speed of the machine slows, but the cadence of pedaling continues at the speed that the rider normally employs on the level. This maintaining of cadence gives the rider maximum use of energy with minimum muscular effort.

If you ride a one-speed bicycle of the old coaster brake, balloon-tire variety, you are denied this advantage; on the uphill grind the pedals slow down until eventually you get off and push. English bicycle makers were thinking about gearing systems in the 1880s, but the inventor who refined the idea and set the stage for the modern gearing equipment was a Frenchman.

Paul de Vivie, a silk merchant until he became deeply interested in bicycles, is rememberd in the bicycle world by his pen name, Velocio. His first bike, acquired when Velocio was twenty-eight, was a high-wheeled model. He rode and practiced on it until he became one of the most skilled riders in his region of France. People watched in awe as he pedaled with astonishing speed and performed tricks on his tall bicycle.

He became so interested in bicycles that eventually he gave up selling silk and turned to working full-time with two-wheelers. In addition to launching his own bicycle publication, de Vivie went into manufacturing in 1889 and began to import high-quality bicycles from other European countries for sale in France. However, none of these bikes would do what he wanted of them on the hills. He realized that if he could change the chain on his machine to sprockets of different sizes, he could alter the gear ratio and give the bicycle added efficiency. His first answer was to make a bicycle with two chain wheels, one smaller than the other.

Lightweight, quick-release sealed hubs with adjustable sealed bearings. AVOCET, INC.

The only way he could switch the chain from one wheel to the other was to get off the bike and make the change by hand. This was the beginning of the derailleur system so widely used today. The obvious next step was for Velocio to make a mechanical device that would shift the chain from one chain wheel to another without the rider having to stop and dismount. Though Velocio accomplished this, he never did bother to take out patents, and, as might be expected, others quickly obtained patents in their own names. There were derailleur-like systems in use in the early years of the present century.

The gear sprockets on the rear hub of a derailleur-equipped bicycle are grouped in a freewheel cluster. In a ten-speed there are five sizes of sprockets in the cluster; in various combinations with the two chainwheels, they give the choice of ten speeds. As the chain changes sprockets, the length of chain required between the two working sprockets changes, and the derailleur must still maintain proper tension. This is accomplished by spring-loaded arms.

WHAT GEARING MEANS

If you look at bicycle advertisements and are confused by the figures that tell you the machine's "gearing," you have a lot of company. These figures, however, are not difficult to understand. What the figures can tell you is the distance the bicycle goes forward, in a given gear setting, with each revolution of the pedals.

This is a holdover from a century ago, when the popular bicycle was one on which the rider

KNOW THE COMPONENT PARTS 45

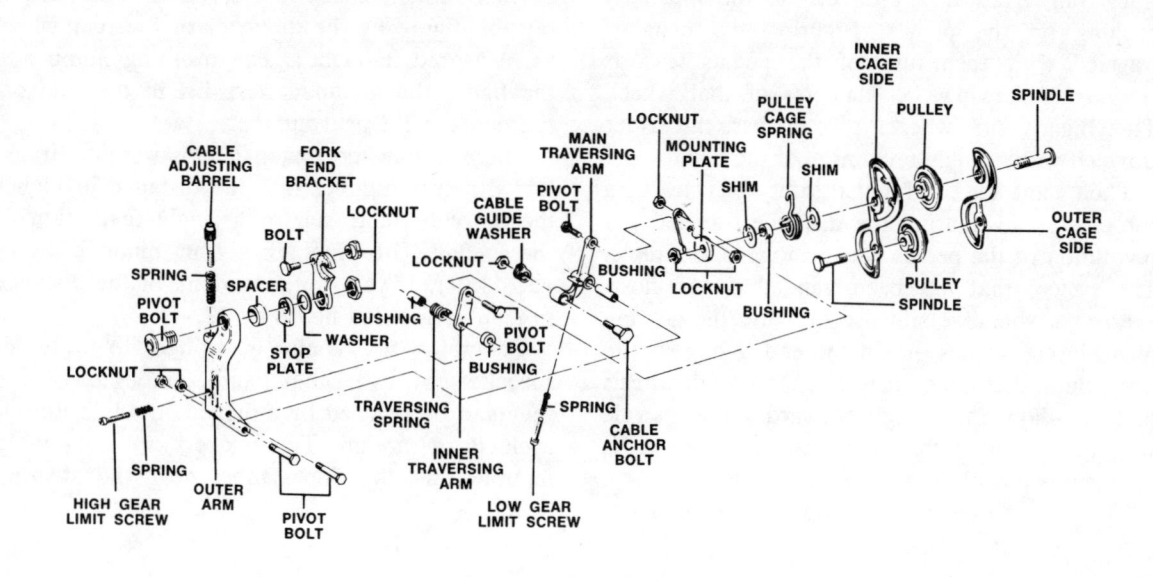

Exploded view of Schwinn-approved rear derailleur. SCHWINN BICYCLE COMPANY.

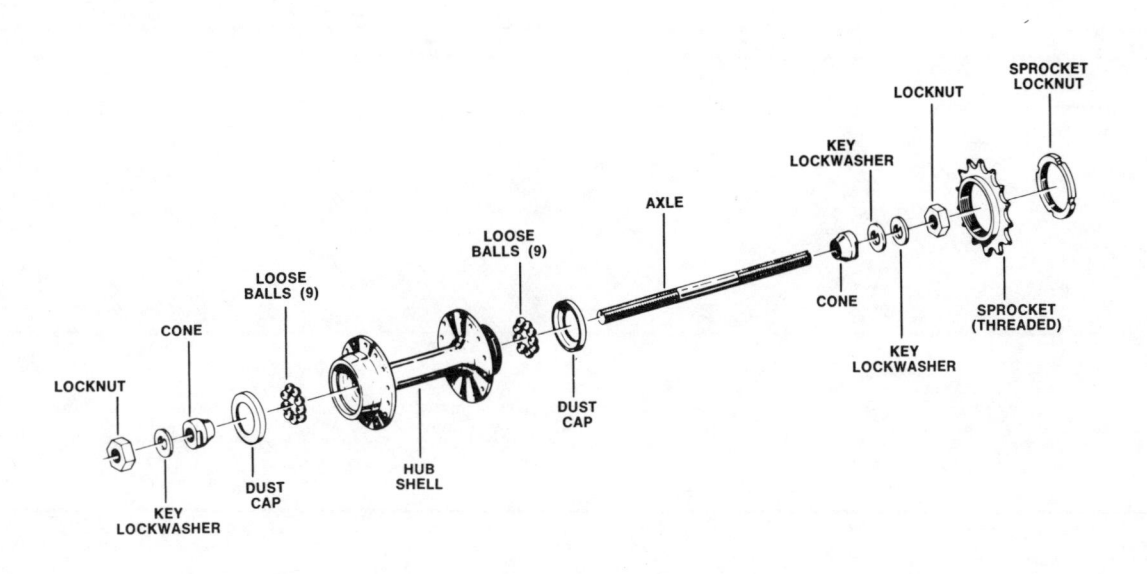

Exploded view of Schwinn-approved fixed rear hub. SCHWINN BICYCLE COMPANY.

perched over the high front wheel. There was no chain or sprocket. Instead, the pedals were built right into the hub of the front wheel and the rider transferred energy directly to the wheel by pushing on the pedals. Figuring the distance traveled with each turn of the pedals was as simple as knowing the diameter of that wheel. The bigger the wheel, the farther the rider traveled with a single revolution of the pedals.

Then came the newfangled safety bicycles with sprockets, and figuring the distance traveled per revolution of the pedals was no longer so simple. The system that has been handed down, however, and which we still use to figure the gearing of a bicycle, comes out in the end telling us the same thing that the diameter of those high wheels told us—how far we go forward on a bicycle with each turn of the pedals when the chain is connecting any of the various sprockets.

This is not difficult to compute once you understand the formula. First you need to know the number of teeth on both front and rear sprockets. Divide the number of teeth on the front sprocket by the number on the rear sprocket. Then multiply this figure by the diameter of the rear wheel as measured in inches. The resulting number is the figure the manufacturers list in their advertisements as the gear number.

There is one more step if you want to translate the gear number into the distance in inches the bicycle will travel for a single revolution of the pedals. Multiply the gear number by π (3.14159). If you prefer to think of the distance in feet, divide that figure by 12.

Generally the chain is shifted to different sprockets by two small handles mounted where they can be reached by either hand while the bicycle is in motion. These levers are commonly mounted on the down tube, near the steering head.

5.

THE ACCESSORIES

The farther you venture from home, the more likely you are to need extra equipment attached to your bicycle. A visit to the bicycle shop can tempt you with all manner of gadgets, but before buying any new item to hang on the bike, you should be convinced that the need is great enough to justify, not only the cost in dollars, but also the cost in energy needed to carry the weight. The basic guideline is to hold extras to a minimum, while equipping your bicycle with those items that really contribute to safety, efficiency and comfort. With this note of caution, you may want to consider the following.

KICKSTANDS

If you join a group of experienced bicycle tourists, you will find that few of them have kickstands on their bikes. These little kick-down rods that are supposed to hold your bike upright when you are not around are widely considered more nuisance than necessity, and for a number of reasons.

First, they add weight. Then, if you try to park on muddy ground, the end of the kickstand sinks in and your bike falls over. They are an unstable support in wind. People brushing past your bike can easily upset it if it is held by a kickstand, and when a bicycle falls down there is always the possibility that the derailleur will be damaged.

In addition, the kickstand is attached to the bike frame by bolting it to the chain stays, and this introduces added threats. It can come loose or, if tightened too forcefully, can be responsible for weakening the chain stays. Bikes that come equipped with kickstands welded on may have been weakened by heat stress at the weld.

You will notice that the highest-quality bicycles come without kickstands for all of these reasons, and that their owners are usually not interested in adding one. Instead of relying on the stand, these cyclists will lean their bikes against a wall or a tree, or lay it on the ground carefully, derailleur side up. If a group travels together, the first rider to stop leans his bike against a tree and the others lean on the first one. To store your bike in the garage, you can hang it from hooks in the ceiling. All of these are better answers to the parking problem than the common kickstand.

Bicycles tend to fall when propped up against stationary surfaces because the front wheel pivots or rolls. Your bicycle shop probably stocks a small, lightweight gadget designed to stabilize the front wheel of parked bikes so they do not fall as readily when leaned and left. Ask for a Flickstand. This lightweight device attaches to the down tube and has a wire that flicks down against the front tire.

Bicycle commuters often equip bicycles with fenders for cleaner riding on wet days. U. S. DEPARTMENT OF TRANSPORTATION PHOTO, JAMES CARROLL.

SAFETY LEVERS FOR BRAKES

The standard levers controlling either side-pull or center-pull caliper brakes are high up on the front of the handlebars. Because this location is sometimes difficult for some riders to reach, a second set of brake levers, called safety levers, may come on a bicycle, or can be installed. If your bicycle has a set of these levers, or you have considered adding them, you should understand that the safety levers might not stop the bike as surely as the standard levers will, and are not always to be trusted. The safety levers ride closer to the handlebars and cannot be pulled as tight as the standard levers. Slight maladjustments in brakes or cables might allow safety levers still less distance over which they can force brake pads to apply pressure against the rims. Most riders are better off without this second set of brake levers.

HANDLEBAR FINGERTIP-CONTROL LEVERS

Riders of ten-speed derailleur-equipped bikes normally have to remove a hand from the handlebars to shift gears. The shift levers are mounted on the frame, usually on the down tube, in such a location that you must lean down to reach them. If you want gear-shift levers closer to your hands, there is an answer—fingertip-control levers on the ends of the handlebars. You can buy these controls from your bicycle shop and either have them installed by the shop's professional mechanic, or install them yourself. Adding handlebar-mounted controls to your bicycle is not a complicated procedure.

FENDERS

Most lower-priced bicycles and children's bicycles leave the factory complete with fenders, while lightweight ten-speed bicycles normally are sold without them. For bicycling around town, however—running errands, riding for pleasure or commuting to school or job—fenders can be highly desirable on rainy days. Admittedly, fenders add some weight, but you can equip the bike with lightweight plastic fenders, or half-fenders that add minimum weight while granting an element of protection to both bike and rider. These are less likely to rattle than the heavier metal fenders, but are more inclined to buckle and break. They are quickly installed if weather looks threatening.

LIGHTS

If you are a serious rider searching for ways to cut weight off the machine, you are going to take a long look at the lights. Perhaps they came with the new bike. But will you need them? Many riders restrict their riding to daylight hours, mak-

THE ACCESSORIES

A good front lamp can be a lifesaving accessory on any bike that is ridden at night. BICYCLE MANUFACTURERS ASSOCIATION OF AMERICA, INC.

Bicycle brake light. Battery-operated light goes on when hand brakes are activated. IMC MANAGEMENT CORP.

ing lamps a burden. When this is realized, the lights are taken off and stuck away in a corner, perhaps permanently.

There are some riders, however, who must have lights. You will need them if you commute during winter months when days are short. Or, if you are a long-distance bicycle tourist, you should be equipped with a light because you can never be sure where the end of the day will catch you.

There are three basic kinds of lights from which to choose: battery-powered lights, generator-powered lights and carbide lamps. Batteries are heavy and they can leak and corrode. This frequently happens if the owner fails to check them periodically, especially when they are not in use. Most bicyclists find it best to remove batteries and put them back when needed.

Generators offer greater dependability as long as the bicycle is moving. Generators are propelled by a roller moving against one of the tires. The safest location for the generator is on the rear wheel where, if it should come loose and get into the wheel, there is less likelihood of a serious accident.

The headlight should be white and plainly visible for at least five hundred feet. The taillight should be red.

In addition, there are lights you can attach to your belt or fasten onto your left arm or leg. These are not substitutes for regular lights, but are excellent supplemental lights.

Some bicyclists carry a standard flashlight in a bracket attached to handlebars or frame. It can be removed when not in use. Touring bicyclists often carry such lights in a pack when they are not actually needed.

Check local and state laws to find out whether lights are required in a specific area.

HORNS

Many experienced bicyclists decide sooner or later that the best horn is no horn. Good defensive riding will keep the rider out of most situations where a horn might be needed. Besides, horns made for bicycles are often so quiet that they cannot be heard in heavy traffic. In addition, they add weight to the bike and tend to break down or wear out after a short life.

One exception is the blast horn operated by Freon escaping from a high-pressure canister. The problem with this one is that it is often too loud. It startles people and, instead of motivating them to give room to the approaching bicycle, might send them scrambling into its path.

The best substitute for a mechanical horn is

the human voice, or a whistle in the case of city riders. If you see that you are getting into a tight spot, or a pedestrian is about to move into your path, give a yell. Shouting "Bicycle!" works better than a horn, and there is no chance of a malfunction.

Parents who want to equip children's bikes with some kind of warning device can settle for those little lever-operated bells that can be attached to the handlebars. These are not going to startle anyone and can help alert pedestrians to the approach of the bicycle.

NAIL REMOVERS

Bits of glass, metal and sharp stones are all trouble for bicycle riders, especially those who have tubulars, or the newer lightweight, high-pressure clincher tires. Bicyclists have developed nail removers that help clean these foreign materials off tubulars before they can become deeply embedded. These nail removers are generally inexpensive devices that attach to the fender or to the caliper brake assembly and permit a wire to ride close to the surface of the tire, scraping off foreign objects. How they are best attached to your bike will depend on the kind of bicycle you ride. But they could save tires, are lightweight and are not much trouble, either to attach to the bike or to keep in place.

MIRRORS

A rider pedaling through this land of the automobile should know not only what is going on in front of the bicycle, but also what is bearing down from the rear. While sounds can alert the rider, details can only be obtained by turning the head and glancing back over the shoulder. In that instant, when the eyes are off the road, the front wheel may ride up on a stone or slip off the edge of the pavement or into a pothole, causing the bicycle to swerve or fall.

The obvious answer is a mirror. Mirrors clamped to the handlebars are another protruding hazard in case of a tumble. A better answer is to equip yourself with one of those postage stamp-size mirrors that fit on a short wire attached to the frame of your glasses or sunglasses.

If you do not wear glasses, these mirrors are also made to attach to the bill of a cap.

This puts the mirror close to the rider's eyes, enabling him or her to observe traffic conditions without turning the head away from the road in front of the bicycle. Some riders do not use mirrors. Some are blessed with better peripheral vision than others. I consider these mirrors well worth their modest cost and any trouble the rider may have getting accustomed to using them. If you ride in traffic, you need some system for seeing the traffic behind your bicycle.

WATER BOTTLE

Dehydration is a problem for cyclists, especially when riding on hot days. Body fluids must be replaced, and the best way to assure this is by carrying water in plastic or aluminum bottles in a cage attached to the frame. This equipment can be found at your bicycle shop.

Keeping water cool on the road is difficult, but warm water is better than none, and if you are sweating it may be better for you than ice water. One method of keeping water cooler without adding much weight is adapted from the experience of desert travelers. A wet cloth sleeve over the water bottle helps cool the water by evaporation. Such sleeves are available commercially, but there is nothing to keep you from making one, even if it is only an old sock fitted over the water bottle. The value is lost, however, as soon as the sleeve dries out.

HOW FAST AND HOW FAR?

Those who want them can buy instruments which, mounted on a bicycle, tell how fast and how far the bicycle goes. You'll find the odometer worth the trouble if you want a more accurate gauge of miles toured than map estimates can give you. These little distance counters are inexpensive. Buy one to match the wheel diameter of your bike.

When I was much younger, I thought the speedometer was also a good piece of equipment to carry up front where I could watch the hand

THE ACCESSORIES

Serious bicyclists equip themselves with small rearview mirrors so they can tell what the traffic is like behind them without having to take their eyes off the road.
BICYCLE MANUFACTURERS ASSOCIATION OF AMERICA, INC.

move as I whisked along. But I have long since decided that how fast I pedal at any given moment is less important than whether or not I feel good. I also came to understand that the speedometer itself can slow a rider down because of its added weight and drag on the wheel. Adults rarely hang speedometers on their bicycles.

BASKETS AND RACKS

Those who use their bicycles for shopping often choose to equip them with wire baskets that fit on the handlebars. These are handy for short trips, but it is better to transport these supplies on a rear carrier. If the handlebars remain free of added weight and bulk, your bicycle will be more easily controlled.

The rear luggage carrier should be ruggedly built and designed so it will not slip. It should be chosen to support the kind of saddlebags or panniers you will carry and to keep them as low as possible, while allowing enough room to insure that your heels do not strike the loaded bags as you pedal. You may want to consider a rear rack that is coated with vinyl as protection against scratching whatever you carry.

Adjustable heavy-duty bike rack fits most bike frames. JIM BLACKBURN DESIGNS.

Aluminum alloy front rack. JIM BLACKBURN DESIGNS.

These racks come in various designs for different jobs. One is equipped with a spring clamp for holding books; if you carry a basketball, you might buy a rack with a hole in the middle that secures the ball as you pedal. Some racks also have special provisions for attaching rear lights or reflectors. The main feature you should look for is rugged, lightweight design so the carrier will support a load over a long period of time without coming loose or rattling. Carriers designed to fit the front of the bicycle are useful if you plan lengthy tours for which you will need more luggage-carrying capacity. These front racks can help balance the load.

For details on packs and panniers, see the section on bicycle camping.

YOUR SPECIAL EQUIPMENT

You may need to equip your bicycle differently from your neighbors' bicycles because of your special interests. If you use the bike to go fishing, ride to band practice or the tennis court or transport a child, you can rig your bike to suit your needs. With the booming interest in tennis there has appeared a special tennis racket clamp that can be attached to the front fork. Many bicycle shops stock it.

Otherwise, you may simply carry your tennis racket, or similar equipment, tied down securely on the rear carrier. Elastic cords with metal hook ends can be especially helpful for carrying books, a jacket, an extra pair of shoes, a briefcase or lunch on the rear carrier.

TOOLS FOR BICYCLE WORK

Everyone who owns a bicycle and rides it is likely to need tools to keep it in good repair. Simply having the right tools on hand encourages a rider to check the bike more frequently. Tools can be especially important if you venture far from home. Mechanical problems can and do occur on tours and the experienced rider will not be caught without the equipment needed to put a disabled bike back on the road, whenever possible. The tools you own for bicycle maintenance and repair can serve equally well on the road or in the home shop, although you will no doubt add tools to the home shop collection that you do not want to carry on the road.

With tool kits, as with everything else you carry, the problem is to take along what you might need and as little else as possible. Tools you keep for other work may also serve for bicycle repairs. If your bicycle is of foreign manufacture, however, or has parts that are foreign-made, you may need metric tools, including a metric Allen wrench set, to service and repair it. One good solution is to start with a basic tool kit available from your bicycle store, such as the kit

For daylong tours in hot weather this cyclist carries a lightweight container of water on the rear carrier of his bike. PHOTO BY THE AUTHOR.

offered by Marfac. This includes a tire repair kit, which always ranks high on any list of bicycle repair equipment. Especially if you are setting off on a long tour, I would consider adding a six- or eight-inch adjustable crescent wrench or a pair of pliers. It is also a good idea to tuck a spoke wrench into your tool kit in case you must replace spokes or tighten them along the route to keep wheels true.

Then, in anticipation of the day you will have to repair a chain, carry another small, low-cost tool—a chain-rivet extractor. Without this tool you may find it next to impossible to make roadside repairs on the chain of a bicycle equipped with derailleurs, because there is no easily removed master link in these chains.

TIRE PUMP

Sooner or later you are going to need a tire pump. Proper inflation is important for easier riding and conservation of energy. Proper inflation also means longer life for tires. Besides, there will come the time when you must repair or replace a tire on the road, and without a pump you will be walking instead of pedaling.

Even where they are available, those powerful pumps used in service stations for automobile tires are bad news for bicycle owners. They make it extremely easy to over-inflate a tire and blow it out.

There are two basic styles of pumps; and you may want one of each. One is the pump you keep in your garage or shop for home use. The other is a smaller pump you carry in a clamp

The rider who carries a hand pump and tire repair kit need not be long delayed by tire troubles.
PHOTO BY THE AUTHOR.

attached to the bicycle frame for roadside use. You will find that bicycle shops offer both kinds in a variety of prices and that quality is generally related to price. A tinny, inexpensive pump may be a poor investment. It is best to buy a more ruggedly built, high-quality pump in the beginning. Check to see that the nozzle on the pump, which is either a Presta or Schraeder type, fits the valves on your tires and, if not, equip yourself with the proper adapter or connector. Also be sure that the pump is capable of fully inflating your tires.

Someone in each group of riders should carry a tire gauge. On tour you will want to check air pressure frequently. The heavier the load on your bike, the more important it is to keep tires inflated to the manufacturer's recommended level.

6. CLOTHING

If your riding is of the fair-weather variety that takes you to the corner store or for an occasional half-hour ride through the nearby park, you probably need no special riding clothes. Use a clip or strap, if needed to keep your pants leg out of the sprocket, and now and then a windbreaker, and you're off and going.

But when you begin taking longer trips, proper clothing becomes important. Color of clothing should provide maximum visibility. There are jackets in brilliant reflector colors made especially for bicyclists. Tests show that bright oranges or yellows give maximum visibility. In general, select light colors over dark.

Bicyclists on long rides wear shorts for freedom of movement. Clothes should fit comfortably and loosely. Even belts should be worn loosely to give maximum comfort and not hinder circulation.

If you are planning your first bicycle tour, the temptation will be to pack too many items of clothing. The more experience you have, the better you can trim your outfit down to essentials. Most touring bicyclists do not need many changes of clothing. For summertime touring you may manage with one change of underwear, socks and shirt, made of material that is easily washed and quickly dried.

If you are subject to sunburn, wear a long-sleeved shirt. Experienced outdoor people know that the secret of being comfortable in cool weather is to wear layers of lighter garments instead of a single heavy one. Rather than a heavy insulated jacket, wear a warm sweater plus a lightweight nylon windbreaker, preferably not a pullover, so it can be worn open as the temperature rises.

Some touring bicyclists like to take clothes for evening wear around camp, hostel or motel. They pack a pair of stay-pressed slacks and a sport shirt, or a wrinkle-resistant skirt and blouse for this purpose.

Packing clothes in panniers to keep them from becoming wrinkled is not impossible. My favorite way to do this is to lay the items out carefully with the creases in place, then roll them. If they are not bulky, underclothes or other soft items can be rolled inside them. Then, pack these rolls upright in the pannier, and you can locate the items you want at any time without unloading the entire pack.

SHOES

Sneakers may seem comfortable at first, but the pressure of feet against rattrap pedals will eventually cause pain on longer rides. A well-broken-in pair of leather shoes may feel right on your feet for short neighborhood rides, but over the long haul heavy shoes add weight. Bicycle tourists and racers find special bicycling shoes more comfortable. Experience has taught them that the solution to the footwear question is a lightweight shoe with a hard sole.

Bicycle shoes may be perforated heavily for ventilation. The soles of some have cleats to fit the shape of the pedals. Racers sometimes wear shoes with lightweight plastic or aluminum cleats, but these are not rugged enough for the touring bicyclist. Standard bicycling shoes are frequently made without heels.

Because these shoes are not for walking, you will need other shoes around camp at the end of the day. A pair of lightweight moccasins or sneakers will serve the purpose. Avocet and Bata shoes, however, combine features of both riding and walking shoes. These might solve the problem of carrying extra shoes on a trip, but they are not hiking shoes.

Riders who find bicycling shoes too costly sometimes settle for a pair of lightweight hiking shoes, then cut grooves in the soles to get a better grip on the pedals. They are hot and heavy, however.

GLOVES

You might not have given much thought to wearing gloves except for cold-weather riding. You will find, however, that bicycle shops stock riding gloves with padded palms and thin, ventilated material on the backs. Touring or racing bicyclists wear these gloves regularly for a good reason: gloves protect the hands from shock. When you ride a lightweight bicycle with turned-down handlebars, the hands help support the body weight and absorb shock. The longer your trip, the more noticeable this becomes. Gloves can also help protect hands in case of a spill. For winter cycling you need warmer gloves, perhaps lined ones. If you ride in bitterly cold weather, you may consider electrically heated gloves. Some riders prefer mittens to regular gloves. Whatever the design, remember that the gloves should be flexible to permit freedom of movement.

HELMETS

There is nothing like an accident to convince a bicyclist that the head should be protected by a hard hat. A friend of mine who made the Bike-

Riding gloves become important as shock absorbers on the hands of touring cyclists. Also, note the use of a protective helmet. PHOTO BY THE AUTHOR.

centennial run across the continent told me that his group went without helmets until one rider had a bad accident and had to quit and go home with a head injury. The group searched out the first bicycle store it could find and all members outfitted themselves with new helmets. They wore them faithfully for the remainder of the trip. A helmet can save your life, and it need not be a burden. Modern helmets are strong but lightweight. They can be bought in sporting goods stores, bicycle shops, motorcycle stores, or stores specializing in safety equipment for industrial use.

Bike riders sweat with or without helmets, but the helmet does aggravate the sweating problem. For this reason, choose one that is designed to give maximum ventilation. For winter use, you can add warm liners and ear muffs and seal the holes in your helmet with tape. Any helmet needs a good chin strap.

Rain pelting against your face or your glasses can obscure vision. A visor on the hat or helmet chosen for touring should give protection against this problem.

CLOTHING

Touring riders carry lightweight, compact rain gear. BICYCLE MANUFACTURERS ASSOCIATION OF AMERICA, INC., PHOTO.

RIDING IN THE RAIN

Touring bicyclists will almost certainly have to travel in the rain. Somewhere along the trail you will need a good outfit to protect yourself against those dark, wet days. The common answer is a poncho or raincoat carried in one of the bags on your bike. These garments, made of modern lightweight materials, take up remarkably little space when packed.

The choice of materials can be important. Thin plastic raincoats do not breathe, they whip wildly in the wind and they can tear easily. They are not going to take hard usage and should be avoided when you are assembling equipment for a bicycle tour. The best material is a tough, lightweight one that will stand up to rain and still "breathe."

The choice of rain gear is a matter of personal preference. For maximum protection you may want a complete rainsuit that covers you from chin to toes. Encased in one of these cocoons, you may find condensation a serious problem, however. Check to see that the jacket has openings beneath the armpits or comparable provisions for ventilation.

If you want to keep feet and legs dry while pedaling, you should check out a special knee-high yellow boot made of lightweight material, designed to slip on over your shoes. Known as "Bike Booties," these are made by Early Winters, Ltd., 100 Prefontaine Place S., Seattle, Washington 98104.

Garbage bags with holes in them for head and arms serve as emergency protection against rain and road dirt. If you are caught on the road on a cold morning without gloves you can utilize a pair of socks as emergency mittens.

7.
LEARNING TO RIDE

Ray Forth of Dayton, Ohio, believes that people are never too old to learn how to ride a bicycle, and the classes he teaches each year provide evidence that he is right. Adults usually don't learn to ride by having a friend run along supporting the bicycle. Forth's procedure involves a more sophisticated method for adult students, although his technique should work for both children and adults.

Teaching a child to ride a bicycle is relatively simple in most families. The first ride should be on a bicycle small enough for the rider to sit on the seat and put both feet on the ground. A three-speed or one-speed coaster brake model will serve better for learning than a fancy ten-speed. A girl's-style frame is best, because the beginner can get off with less chance of falling.

For teaching the young child I prefer giving the lesson on a smooth lawn instead of on a paved surface. A slight downgrade to the lawn gives the beginner a little more speed and makes the initial balancing easier. The paved surface provides a smoother ride, but on the grass the child senses that a fall, if it should happen, is less likely to bang up knees and elbows.

The actual procedure is simplicity itself. After getting the child onto the bicycle, the instructor, holding on to the bicycle all the while, walks along beside it as the student learns to balance by "scootering" the bike with his feet. When the student begins to pedal, the work is gradually transferred from the instructor's arms to the student's legs, and the new rider begins to sense that he is moving under his own power.

When the rider is doing the work and seems able to maintain balance, the adult can remove his hand from the seat. In gradual steps the new rider has learned to maintain his balance and to make the machine go. From there on, even though there may be a spill or two ahead, the learning progresses rapidly with practice.

Most of Forth's students are over forty years old, although the actual age span is from twenty to seventy-two years. One woman past seventy took his course, bought a new bicycle and began riding regularly. Another student in her fifties became so proficient that she signed up for the TOSRV (Tour of the Scioto River Valley) and completed this famous Ohio 200-mile weekend ride with no mishaps, although she had had only two years' riding experience. Forth admits that some of his students give up if they decide they are not up to the physical challenge. More than 80 per cent of those who start, however, go on to complete the training and learn how to ride.

This project began when Forth, as president of the Dayton Cycling Club, decided that the club should initiate riding instruction for adults. He learned that the Chicago Wheelmen already had a program started, and a delegation of Dayton club members went to Chicago to go through the learning sessions. They returned with the instructions on tape. Forth then went to the Montgomery County Parks and Recreation Depart-

LEARNING TO RIDE

Children learn to ride bicycles quickly. The rider should look ahead and pedal while getting a hand from an older instructor (top left). Supporting the bicycle, not the child (right), the instructor runs along beside the new rider until confidence and ability enable the rider to pedal off alone (bottom left). ROSS BICYCLES PHOTOS.

ment, in Dayton, with his plan. "We wanted them to sponsor the program," he explains, "and we would do the teaching. This way, no matter who came and went within the club, the county sponsorship would give the program continuity. In addition, they would have the responsibility for hauling the training bicycles to and from the parks and schools where the training sessions were held. "I would strongly recommend," says Forth, "that anyone starting such a program set it up this way."

Selling the plan to the county was not difficult. "We told them what Chicago had learned," he says. When Chicago set up its training program, the schedule was announced in the newspapers. Three thousand people joined up. The teachers, who had hoped to handle the instruction on a one-to-one basis, were temporarily swamped. The Dayton program signed up twenty-one students for the first session, with five members of the cycling club serving as instructors.

Based on Chicago's experience, Forth knew what kind of bicycles were best for teaching. The first requirement was that the bike should be women's style for ease of mounting and dismounting. The second choice would have been a mixte frame. It should have drop handlebars and hand brakes. Beyond that, the bicycle could have any number of speeds.

The steps followed in this course will also work without an instructor, for the person determined to learn how to ride. The Dayton course is

Bicycle instructor Ray Forth, who says "You are never too old to learn to ride," starts older beginners out on a bicycle with one pedal removed and the seat reversed. PHOTO BY THE AUTHOR.

Bicycles are popular in retirement villages because they offer convenience in running errands and a pleasant way to exercise. BICYCLE MANUFACTURERS ASSOCIATION OF AMERICA, INC., PHOTO.

divided into eight weekly two-hour classes, almost all of it spent in practicing each lesson.

For the first session, Forth turns the saddle backward, because at this stage he does not want the student using it and it should be out of the way. He then removes the right pedal because the rider has to keep one foot on the ground. "First," says Forth, "you lean the bicycle over and learn to step through." The student then places the left foot on the pedal at the six o'clock position. Using the right foot for balance, the beginner moves along, scooterlike, in a half-hop, half-coast.

One additional important procedure at this stage involves the position of the hands. Forth wants the right hand on the low part of the handlebar and the left hand on the top. Keeping balance this way requires that the weight be on the right side, supported by the right foot on the ground. Any fall is likely to be in that direction, and all the person must do to recover is step through the bike frame.

These sessions are on a paved surface where there is no traffic. The first of the eight two-hour sessions is spent practicing this single procedure, learning how the bicycle feels when balanced and learning how to use the brakes.

The second lesson allows the student to get both feet off the ground. Instead of hopping along on the right foot, the rider lifts the body weight onto the left foot and coasts with the right foot slightly off the ground.

At the beginning of the third session the seat is turned back to its correct position. The right pedal is still not back on the bike. Now the student sits on the saddle. The riding at this point is a single downstroke, then coasting, another downstroke and coasting. "A slight downgrade helps," says Forth.

By this time the student should be balancing well, so for lesson four the right pedal is replaced, and for the first time the rider actually begins pedaling. The last four sessions consist of more practice and personal instruction while the student gains confidence and learns how to handle a bicycle under different road conditions.

Learning to ride may be easier for you. Not all people are born equal when it comes to a sense of balance.

Once the beginner learns the rudiments and gains skill and confidence in riding, a few of the finer points will become important. There is a correct way to mount your new ten-speed, and it is best to learn this procedure from the beginning. One does not put a foot, cowboy fashion, into the stirrup and throw oneself into the saddle. Instead, begin by straddling the top tube. Then put the left foot on the pedal, which should be at the 10 o'clock position. Toe clips help the rider keep the balls of the feet on the pedals, instead of permitting the arch to rest on the pedal in what would be a highly inefficient and tiring foot position.

If you are learning to ride with toe straps, keep them loose. (They should be loose when riding in traffic anyway, because you may want to get your feet out of them in a hurry.) With your left foot in place as you straddle the top tube, push off with the right foot, push down on the left pedal, and pull yourself into the saddle, all in one smooth, fluid motion. Do it this way every time and the proper method soon becomes automatic.

Using rattrap pedals and toe clips, you can begin to practice the important technique of ankling. This is a method of controlling the position of the feet to gain maximum use of leg and foot muscles. The experienced rider knows that powering a bicycle involves more than simply pushing down on each pedal as it comes into position. You should gain power not only from pushing through that first half of the cycle starting at the 12 o'clock position, but also by pulling the pedal up with the toes (ankling). This steady pressure makes for a more even and restful ride. It is possible because, with feet strapped to the pedals, you can apply pressure both by pushing down on the ball of the foot and by lifting with the toes. When practicing ankling, try to check the foot position at various points in its revolution. The foot should be flat as you push down. The toes should be slightly below the heel on the upstroke. Then, by the time the foot reaches the 10 o'clock position, the heel is coming back to a position level with the toe.

Ray Forth, who also teaches bicycle riding classes at the University of Dayton, has his university students practice ankling by taking one foot off the pedal. "Pedaling with just one foot," he says, "they have to lift as well as push, and they soon begin to understand the proper foot position." Ankling may seem taxing at first, but

Bicyclists riding on unpaved roads must be especially careful to avoid stones, holes and other obstacles that might damage tires. MAINE DEPARTMENT OF COMMERCE AND INDUSTRY PHOTO.

with practice the proper ankle motion becomes almost automatic. It could well be the single most important technique you will learn about riding a bicycle, and the more you ride, the more important ankling will become.

Good riders do not pedal fast, then slow, then coast, then pedal fast again. Instead they attempt to keep the revolutions of the crank at about the same number per minute throughout the ride, establishing a "cadence," which my dictionary defines as a rhythmic sequence. A bicycle rider's cadence is the number of times per minute he or she can turn the crank comfortably, a figure that differs greatly from rider to rider, though an average is somewhere between seventy and eighty strokes per minute. What your natural cadence might be is less important than maintaining that "rhythmic sequence." As you go either up or down grades, instead of altering the speed at which you turn the crank, you use gears to help maintain your cadence.

WATCH ROAD SURFACES

You can save yourself trouble by learning to watch the road ahead of you and spotting obstacles and hazards before you are upon them. You will see areas that seem to be slick, wet or strewn with loose gravel or dirt while there is time to avoid them. If you find yourself riding through such an area, never panic and attempt to swerve out of it; the sudden change in direction can put you into a slide from which you can't recover. Sudden changes in speed are also inadvisable if you are trying to avoid sliding. It's better to keep firm control of the machine and attempt to maintain both speed and direction until you have ridden onto clean road again.

Early spring riding can be especially hard on bicycles, since the winter cycles of freezing and thawing can break up the hard road surface, leaving jagged edges and potholes. On some roads it is impossible to miss all the rough places. You may be better off to walk your bike around such areas rather than risk destroying a tire or bending a wheel. Watch also for sewer grates and railroad tracks, which can throw you or damage your bicycle. If you ride over railroad tracks, cross at a right angle.

With experience you will find that you can give your bike a softer ride over the rough places by the way you adjust your weight on it. When the going is rough, try leaning forward, lifting some of the weight off the saddle so you put some spring in your bent arms and legs and take up some of the shock the bike would otherwise absorb.

Curbs are a menace. Riding close to them when going slow is especially hazardous. Hitting a curb can break tire sidewalls and bend rims. The same thing can happen if you purposely ride over curbs or carelessly bounce from a driveway onto the street.

Good riders travel in a straight line. The bicycle that wobbles or weaves wastes your energy. Riding in a straight line is more easily accomplished if you apply pressure to the pedals smoothly, not erratically. The skilled rider and the bike become a single unit as the rider grows increasingly sensitive to the movements of the bicycle. This sensitivity toward the bicycle improves efficiency and adds to the pleasures of riding.

8. TRANSPORTING THE BICYCLE

If a person never had to put a bicycle on a van or a car, both the owner and the bicycle would be better off. But motor vehicles transport bikes to where they are most useful, whether it be to the edge of town or to a distant vacation spot. Because they cannot fit inside most vehicles and leave room for all of the other equipment, bicycles must normally be attached, in some manner, to the outside of the car. The choice of location depends on the vehicle design and the owner's preference. On recreational vehicles the bike rack may ride better on the front. Besides, the spare tire or a rear-opening door may make the back of the vehicle unsuitable for a bike rack. In any case, the driver must constantly keep the attached bicycles in mind, especially when parking. (This seems the appropriate place to offer the usual advice about not backing into a low-clearance garage, forgetting that the bicycles are topside.)

If you are buying a car rack for bicycles, there are some important points worth considering. First is the number of bicycles you will be carrying. If you are carrying more than two, the best place for them is probably on top of your vehicle. There are racks designed to go over the automobile trunk which can carry up to four bicycles. Some cartop racks can carry four or even five bicycles. A bumper-supported rack is generally good for one or two bicycles, seldom more.

Make sure that parts of the rack in contact with your bicycles are covered with vinyl or other protective material that will prevent marring the bicycle's paint. Search for racks made or treated with materials that will prevent corrosion and give them longer life.

But above all, check to see that the rack you are considering will fit your vehicle. Some are designed to fit any car, station wagon or van of foreign or domestic manufacture. Some rack makers, taking into consideration the tailgates and trunk lids, have designed their carriers so they do not have to be removed to give access to the vehicle or trunk. This is a feature worthy of consideration.

Also, you may consider whether or not the rack can be used in a garage or basement for bicycle storage. If you ski, you can choose a rack that will do double duty by carrying bicycles in summer and skis in winter.

You can also make your own cartop rack. Start with a pair of cartop carriers, substantial ones that can be fastened securely. Cut a pair of wooden bars to fit across the carriers. The bicycles should ride upside down on the rack, parallel to the road. Notches cut into the crossbars, or attached blocks, secure the handlebars and saddles. Take special care to prevent damage to control cables. The crossbars should be covered with carpeting or with rubber from old inner tubes to protect bike surfaces. When mounting a bicycle on a rack, it is good practice to protect painted surfaces by separating them with cloth or strips of carpeting.

Vacationers who take their bicycles along can explore countless state and national parks, forest areas and wildlife refuges. WASHINGTON STATE TRAVEL PHOTO.

Bike caddy with plastic-coated arms carries two bicycles. J.C.I. BICYCLE PRODUCTS.

Circle caddy carries one or two bicycles; bumper-mounted. J.C.I. BICYCLE PRODUCTS.

Bumper-mounted cycle caddy carries two bicycles. J.C.I. BICYCLE PRODUCTS.

Unless you have a system for holding the bike in place, it may tumble right off the rack before you can tie it down securely. A strap, or a band of old inner tube attached so it fits across the handlebars, will hold the bikes while you finish tying them down. You can rig leather straps with buckles or heavy strips of inner tube to secure both handlebars and saddles during travel.

When you use this kind of cartop carrier, you can accommodate more bikes by alternating the direction they face when mounted on the rack.

A little practice in hoisting a bicycle to the top of the car will smooth out the procedure. After removing pump, water bottle and other such items, I stand the bike between myself and the car, facing the same way it will in transit. Then I reach across it and swing the wheels up and away from me so I can settle the handlebars and the saddle into their notches on the carrier bars.

Before starting on any trip, double-check the bike carrier to see that it is secure, that there is no wobbling and that all parts are snugly in place. Then, at each stop, give the rack a quick inspection to be certain nothing has worked loose.

One of my friends, now in his sixties, carries his bike and his wife's bike inside their van whenever they leave on a trip of any significant length. First the table in the van is lifted off its single leg and stored so the two bikes can be tied to the table leg.

Once this outfit is at the destination, which might be a city or state park or a special bike trail, the bikes are out and ready to go in less

The fun of bicycling includes riding with friends. BICYCLE MANUFACTURERS ASSOCIATION OF AMERICA, INC., PHOTO.

than a minute. "It is quicker and easier than hanging the bikes on racks," he says, "and it keeps them free of the mud and dirt that would get on them outside." Still, this system is not for everyone. As my van-driving friend admits, "The bikes have to come out of the van before we can fix our bed for the night, or even before we can set up the table for a roadside lunch stop."

Besides, vans, especially those carrying several children, are usually loaded down with other belongings, leaving precious little room on the inside for anything bike-size.

PUBLIC TRANSPORT

Public transportation companies have widely varying rules and rates pertaining to shipment of bicycles. Furthermore, rules change frequently. The airline companies could simplify the whole process by standardizing their regulations. This may happen. But, as long as there remain many sets of regulations, the touring bicyclists planning to make part of the trip by plane, boat, bus or rail should check with each individual carrier as plans for the trip mature and the modes of transportation are chosen.

Some airlines consider the bicycle a piece of baggage that can be substituted for one of the allowed suitcases on the regular ticket. An informal survey turned up the following information on shipping bicycles.

Delta Airlines, Inc., says that, because of the special handling needed, a bicycle is not considered part of a passenger's free baggage allowance. The traveler checking a bicycle can expect, as this is written, to pay $12 as a one-way fare for the machine on any domestic or international trip, except trans-Atlantic flights. The bicycle rate, one way, to Frankfurt, Germany, is $45, and to London, $35. For shipping by Delta, your bicycle must be crated in a cardboard container (provided free) or else handlebars and pedals must be encased in styrofoam with pedals removed and handlebars turned sideways. "But," warns Delta, "these conditions can change. Check with your local Delta office."

According to a spokesman for Alaska Airlines, "Bicycles are carried routinely on our flights." Alaska Airlines charges a $10 fee and does not count the bicycle as normal baggage. The traveler must turn the handlebars parallel to the frame and remove the pedals. Cartons are not provided or required, but are recommended.

Eastern Airlines, Inc., has regulations similar to those of Alaska Airlines, but requires the use of cartons, which "you may obtain from skycaps at the airport." This is not always as easily done as the airline indicates, and if you need a cardboard carton for shipping your bike, it is sound planning to call the airport ahead of time and make sure the cartons are available. Bicycle shops frequently have cartons on hand and may give you one.

United Airlines charges $12 for shipping a bicycle and requires the owner to crate the bicycle in a carton supplied by the airline, after turning handlebars sideways and removing pedals.

TWA permits its overseas passengers on trans-Atlantic flights to substitute a bicycle for one of the allowed free bags, and makes the usual excess baggage charge if the total shipped exceeds the standard baggage allowance. TWA charges $12 for transporting a bicycle on domestic flights and does not include them in regular baggage allowances.

Most airlines suggest that travelers planning to take along a bicycle allow at least one hour of extra time at the airport for check-in.

If you are going by Greyhound Bus, you can check your bicycle as baggage, but to take advantage of this offer, the bicycle must be transported in a wood, leather or canvas carrying case, no larger than 8"×32"×60", all securely fastened with ropes or straps. If you want to ship your bicycle by bus and meet it at the destination, this too can be arranged. The rules and shipping charges (which vary with the trip) should be checked with your local Greyhound office.

Bagging bicycles for airline shipment is rapidly gaining popularity over packing them in cartons. Bicyclists, on occasion, have built special crates to protect their machines in transit. These, however, are invariably heavy and usually cumbersome to handle. There is also the problem of what to do with the crate once you reach your destination.

One of my neighbors was planning to fly to Florida with his eleven-year-old son to ride around Homestead and the Everglades National Park during the League of American Wheelmen's Winter Rendezvous. His first thought was to crate the bicycles, but after a talk with a seasoned bicycle traveler, he decided on a rugged canvas bag manufactured by the Bike Bag Company, 7475 West 16th Avenue, Lakewood, CO 80215.

Packing the bicycles was simple: pedals were removed, handlebars were left in riding position, and both wheels were taken off for storage in special sections of the bag. Instead of an unwieldy carton, each bike was now in a package one person could handle.

In addition, the bike bag, containing a bicycle as well as some spare clothing, could be slung from a shoulder and carried to the check-in counter. There it was processed as regular baggage and shipped without added cost.

The bike bag is an excellent solution, especially for machines with quick-release wheels. At the destination the carrying bag can be rolled and packed on the carrier.

When the Florida-bound bicyclists arrived at Miami International Airport, they watched with some misgivings as the luggage came to the pick-up area. Fragile equipment packed with all those cases and boxes can be easily damaged. The bike bags, however, are bright orange and labeled, so the chances are excellent that they will not be packed under heavy freight or carried where they will shift position and get crushed. The two bicycles were delivered in perfect condition.

While this information gives the bicyclist a good indication of what is involved in shipping the bicycle, the matter should still be checked with the airline, boat or railroad company well ahead of time as a regular part of planning for the trip.

9.
THOSE BIG RIDES

During the bicycling season there are hundreds of organized rides, especially in the more heavily populated regions of the country. One way to keep abreast of planned events in which you might want to participate is to join a local bicycle club. Most clubs plan a variety of rides—short, long, easy, difficult. Bicycle shops often post notices of upcoming rides, or else a member of the sponsoring group comes around to leave a stack of notices beside the cash register where riders can see them. Some bicycle clubs get notices of their upcoming events in local newspapers. If there is a bicycle rental agency in the community, the operator probably knows about rides planned for the area.

If you are a member of the League of American Wheelmen, you know that affiliated clubs list many of their national rides in the L.A.W. Bulletin. Each issue carries several pages of these notices, with details on dates, times of departure, fees charged, kind of terrain and length of ride, plus information on accommodations.

Some rides are so well known locally that you are almost certain to hear about them if you ride and live within a convenient distance. Several years ago, for example, the Dayton, Ohio, Cycling Club initiated its Huffman 100, and every May this popular ride is repeated with a mass start at 8 A.M., rain or shine. Sanctioned by the League of American Wheelmen and typical of many such rides, this event is planned for the fun of riding, not as a test of endurance. If a rider wants to cover only twenty-five or fifty of the 100 miles, the route can be altered to suit his goals. The route leads through beautiful farming country with gentle hills, every turn is marked, and each rider is given a map for guidance. In short, this ride, like many others around the country, is made easy to follow and easy to enjoy whether the rider is a beginner or an expert. Much of the fun of these organized rides comes from meeting other riders and having the opportunity to trade bicycle talk and experiences.

Typically also, the Huffman 100 has a modest registration fee. In exchange, the rider receives, not only the appropriate patches to indicate participation, but also snack stops and the service of sag wagons that rescue those whose bicycles break down or muscles give out.

If you are in Iowa, in the heart of America, on a certain summer day, you can join several thousand other bicyclists as they start out on that state's biggest bicycle event, a seven-day tour across the entire state.

Iowa's big bicycle ride began when two staff writers from the Des Moines *Register* planned to cross the state by bicycle and send back daily dispatches about their experiences. Word spread, and by the time the reporters started nearly 300 riders were ready to join them. Everyone had a memorable time and the ride was repeated the next year with 2,800 riders participating.

The Iowa ride, called RAGBRAI for *"Register*'s Annual Great Bike Ride Across Iowa," is one of the least organized rides in the country.

Among the most famous distance rides in the United States is the annual Tour of the Scioto River Valley, a double century held on Mother's Day weekend which draws thousands of bicyclists from all over the United States and abroad to the rural roads between Columbus and Portsmouth, Ohio. TOSRV PHOTO.

The route stretches four hundred miles, from west to east, permitting the prevailing winds from the west to give riders a boost. Riders are on their own and there is no registration fee. Farmers grant camping privileges. Villages provide access to showers and swimming pools. School buildings are opened for those who need lodging. Details are available from the promotion department of the Des Moines *Register,* 715 Locust Street, Des Moines, IA 50304.

Perhaps the best-known group distance ride in the country starts once a year in Columbus, Ohio. It gets underway shortly after dawn on the Saturday morning of Mother's Day weekend. On one of these rides recently, Charley Pace settled himself on his ten-speed on High Street in front of Ohio's State House in the center of Columbus and headed south. Riding with him was a ham radio operator whose bicycle was equipped with the best in two-way radio equipment. This two-man team was the control unit.

Other riders were funneling onto High Street. For more than an hour they continued to mount their bikes and turn south. The road was lined with riders, all headed for Portsmouth on the Ohio River, 106 miles away. People living along the route would see riders throughout the day, a seemingly endless string of bicycles moving steadily down the Scioto River Valley through southern Ohio's hills. The following day they would see them coming back on the second lap of this famous ride. Every year since 1962, they have watched the bicycles on Mother's Day weekend.

When this route was first ridden, the bicyclists had no idea that they were founding what would become a bicycling classic. Greg Siple and his father made the run alone that year. Their only reason was that they thought it would make an interesting ride.

The next year the Siples decided they would repeat the ride. This time, eight of their friends wanted to go along. The third year there were thirty-four. One of them was Charley Pace, who divided his spare time between bicycling and canoeing. The annual ride was rapidly becoming a tradition, and each year the number of participants increased as word of the event spread.

Any ride involving this many people calls for organization—a lot of it. Charley Pace fell into the job of managing the event, which came to be known as the Tour of the Scioto River Valley—TOSRV.

This river valley provides an excellent setting for such a ride for several reasons. The country offers an exceptionally pleasant rural landscape of rolling green farmlands where riders cross little creeks and ride back roads between fields of corn and green pastures. The Scioto Valley is also rich in history: it is the home of the mysterious mound builders, the land of Tecumseh and Chief Logan, the site of numerous conflicts between Indians and pioneers. It is, in sum, a fine, pleasant land in which to ride on a spring weekend, if you hit the weather right.

The route is not too difficult for the average rider who stays in shape, and there are towns along the way where one can stop and rest.

The TOSRV has grown to what Pace considers its capacity. "We had thirty-five hundred and seventy register this year," he told me. "Some drop out, but about thirty-three hundred started. Usually around eighty-three per cent finish the ride. That means bicyclists are riding eight hundred thousand miles in the Valley over the Mother's Day weekend."

Pace is scarcely closing the records on one year's TOSRV before he is working again on the next one. Most of his time, when he is not busy at the Columbus bank where he works as an investment officer, now goes into the annual ride. "It couldn't be done at all," he once told me, "if it were not for all the volunteer help we get." The ride is sponsored by the Columbus Council of American Youth Hostels.

Among the riders are bicyclists from more than thirty states, including Alaska. Riders from South Africa and France fly in, with their bicycles, especially for this ride. Pace's efforts to keep this more than an Ohio ride have obviously succeeded.

Large numbers of riders return year after year to ride with friends they have not seen since the year before. "Two-thirds of them are repeaters," Charley Pace told me. "We had five hundred and thirty who had made the tour six or more times. Why? I don't know why they do it. I've asked some of them and don't seem to get good answers."

For five months before the tour, volunteer helpers of the AYH are busy answering mail and processing applications. An astounding number of people volunteer their efforts to make this tour a success. The radio contact that Pace is able to maintain as he pedals along the mapped route is possible because sixty volunteers work in the radio network. Twenty or more paramedics from Ohio National Guard and Red Cross units cruise the route. There is usually medical aid available within minutes if a rider gets into trouble. Altogether some five hundred volunteers are on hand.

There has never been a fatal accident on the TOSRV, although every year brings a few injuries. One rider, speeding across a bridge, rode off the edge and broke a shoulder. If a rider has an accident and becomes unconscious, that person can immediately be identified by a number worn on the clothing. All records are on computers and the number tells Pace the rider's name and

These riders are off at dawn on the annual tour of the Scioto River Valley. PHOTO BY THE AUTHOR.

home address almost instantly. Pace, riding along at 14 to 18 miles an hour, quickly gets a CB report on any injury and how it is being handled.

All the food is prepared and handled by volunteers. Pace buys the food, paying for it from the registration fees. He purchases five hundred dozen doughnuts, seventy boxes of apples, seventy boxes of oranges, seven hundred loaves of bread and nine hundred and fifty pounds of bananas. Women in Portsmouth cook and serve the riders more than three thousand chicken dinners, paid for from the registration fees. Food stops are spotted along the route. Pace likes to call it "the biggest progressive dinner in the world."

He sees the modest registration fee as one of the biggest bargains in the travel world. The fee covers hauling overnight baggage to Portsmouth and back, eight food stops, a chicken dinner on Saturday night when they arrive and floor space in a gymnasium in Portsmouth for sleeping. Those arriving in Columbus the day before the tour starts are given space to sleep in a building at the State Fair grounds.

There is no special pressure on riders who make this tour. You travel at your own best speed. Strong bicyclists may arrive in Portsmouth early in the afternoon. Others take the entire day to make the first leg of the two-hundred-mile trip.

Most of the bicycles are ten-speeds, but there is variety among them. Some riders pedal five-speed bikes, others push along on single-speed machines. There are always several tandems. Among the riders are eight- and ten-year-olds, as well as a sprinkling of elderly riders. "The oldest one this year," Pace reported, "was a man who was seventy-four, and he didn't have any trouble." Many make it a family ride.

The gear is hauled in a fleet of seven twenty-two-foot U-Haul trucks. A family of 16 people regularly volunteer to drive the trucks and handle packs. It is their way of getting together on Mother's Day.

The TOSRV is not a trip to be approached without experience or conditioning. It is a lot of pedaling in two days. I once asked Charley Pace to tell me from his experience what advice he would give those who might be thinking of making the TOSRV trip for the first time. "Get in condition," he said quickly. "This should not be the first long tour a rider makes. He should have ridden a hundred-mile ride before and know he can make it." This ride comes early in the year, when some riders are not yet in top condition.

RIDING THE CENTURY

To bicyclists, a "century ride" means covering one hundred miles in a day, and it is a special accomplishment, particularly the first time it is done. An L.A.W.-sanctioned century is 100 miles in 12 hours or less. If you are young and filled with energy, this may not seem to be an overwhelming challenge. At the end of the ride, however, you may look upon the century with considerably more respect. It is a test of staying power, and a ride for which you should be in good condition. For most of us, this means it should come late in the bicycling season, preferably near the end of summer, after the weather has begun to cool off somewhat.

Century rides are scheduled by clubs all over the country every year. Clubs associated with the League of American Wheelmen sponsor many of them, especially in September, which the L.A.W. calls its national century month. These group rides are a good way to tackle your first century ride. Experienced riders can give helpful tips to the newer riders. Besides, you will have company part of the time, as well as the added impetus of knowing that other riders with you are aiming at the same goal.

I am not going to tell you flat out never to consider a long ride on a bicycle with fewer than ten speeds, but there is no doubt that you increase your odds of completing what otherwise might be a grind and enjoying the trip if you have a properly fitted ten-speed bicycle to ride. The high-pressure tires, lighter weight and choice of gears all work in your favor, as does the riding position with dropped handlebars. The bicycle should be in top condition, with tires fully inflated.

Wind resistance is one of the factors you should consider in planning your trip. Also worth remembering is that the less extra weight you carry, the easier the hill riding will be. Trim the burden to essentials.

Whether you are purposely setting forth to ride a century, or are off on a tour that will keep you traveling in day-long sessions, the preconditioning is similar. Work up to the day of departure with a training program that builds strength and stamina. Consult with your doctor in advance, especially if you are past thirty-five, and have a thorough physical if you are looking ahead to your first long tour or century ride.

10.
THE BIKE TRAILS ARE WAITING

In recent years thousands of miles of new bicycle routes have been marked, new bike lanes have been set aside and completely new trails have been constructed. Bikeways are being linked together in an ever-widening system that promises to grow in the years ahead because the demand is growing, and because government agencies are beginning to understand that bicyclists need more and better places to ride.

Most states have some designated bikeways. Contact with your state department of transportation or natural resources will generally lead to information on bicycle trails near you. The idea of selecting suitable routes for bicycles and marking them started in Homestead, Florida, where George and Nadine Fichter were concerned about the safety of children riding on the streets. There were quiet streets where motor vehicle traffic was of low volume. Why not find the safest routes for Homestead bicyclers and have them labeled as bike routes? The Fichters began rounding up help and consulting with city officials, the board of education and citizen groups. Meanwhile Homestead cyclists rode their streets, locating those safest for bicycle riding. The designated streets connected homes with schools, playgrounds and shopping areas, and the new bicycle routes were clearly marked with new signs. This pioneering bicycle route was dedicated in 1962, and within months the idea was spreading beyond Homestead. Here was an idea whose time had come. Not only were the bike routes safer for children, but they provided recreational routes for adult cyclists, whose numbers were growing every day. In the following years a wide variety of new bicycle routes appeared, as some of the more enlightened government administrators and traffic engineers included the bicycle in their planning. The drive for more and better bike routes is still on.

Those who work with bikeways speak of three classes of bike routes, generally described as follows:

Class I. These are trails separated from highways. They may run parallel to highways or streets, but between the bike route and the street there is either a space or a physical barrier. These routes are often used by pedestrians and sometimes by skateboarders as well.

Class II. These are designated bike routes that are part of highways or streets, but are set off by painted lines or low barriers.

Class III. These are routes bicycles share with motor vehicles. They are usually chosen partly because of the relative scarcity of motor vehicles that use them, and are marked with "Bike Route" signs.

Some bicycle routes have become widely known among riders. Here is a sampling of noted rides that are popular in various parts of the country.

Beginning in 1967, Wisconsin hit on what turned out to be an excellent idea for developing bike trails. The state acquired thirty-two miles of an abandoned railroad between Elroy and Sparta. "At first," one state official told me, "we

This family equipped with bicycles has found a quiet street where the traffic is light—ideal for cycling. BICYCLE MANUFACTURERS ASSOCIATION OF AMERICA, INC., PHOTO.

Transportation planners are giving increasing attention to bicycle trails that separate cyclists and motorists. BICYCLE MANUFACTURERS ASSOCIATION OF AMERICA, INC., PHOTO.

thought it would just be used for a backpacking trail."

Before long, however, bicyclists discovered the Elroy-Sparta State Trail, and soon they were outnumbering hikers, although both still use it. Wisconsin estimates that 48,000 bicyclists a year use this trail. "We've had riders from every state in the union," I was told, "from all over Canada and some other countries too." In Wisconsin they are no longer surprised to see bicyclists from distant places arrive to ride this trail, and Wisconsin officials think they know why.

One reason is that the old roadbed built for train use offers gentle grades—maximum 3 per cent. "This makes it an easy, pleasant ride," I heard more than once, "the kind of trail older riders and families can enjoy."

In addition, the landscape is rural and scenic. Wisconsin's dairy farm country is perhaps the greenest this side of Ireland—may Vermont forgive me. Herds of cattle graze the rolling fields. Streams wind through the countryside. The trail crosses thirty-three trestles. Favorite trail features include the three long tunnels built through solid

Trails shared by bicyclists and pedestrians are better ridden at a leisurely pace than at high speed. U. S. DEPARTMENT OF TRANSPORTATION PHOTO, JAMES CARROLL.

rock for trains and now turned over to cyclists. Their ceilings are still black from the smoke of the engines. Flashlights are needed if your bike is not light-equipped. One of these tunnels is seven-tenths of a mile long.

Then there are the people in the villages along the way. They seem not to grow tired of their bicycling visitors, even after many years. One farmer invites riders to stop and see his modern milking operation. Another is known for the stories he tells. There are four modest-sized villages along the trail where riders stop for supplies and refreshments. Perhaps one reason they are welcome is that a sophisticated study by the state shows that bicyclists bring $269,000 a year into these communities in new money they would otherwise not have. This should be a strong argument to motivate other communities to develop bicycle trails.

Many come to the Elroy-Sparta Trail for a weekend of riding, leaving their cars at one end and pedaling a round trip on the trail at a leisurely pace. Others go for a one-day ride, leaving cars at both ends or arranging for a local shuttle service to transport them back to their starting point. Those who want to rent bicycles and ride the trail can arrange this at the old railroad station about midway along the trail.

There are campgrounds operated by the state at either end of the trail, as well as privately operated campgrounds along the way. There is also a campground about midway, at Wilton. This is a

This sign points bicyclists to quiet and pleasant corners of America. HUFFMAN MANUFACTURING COMPANY.

popular stop, perhaps in part because the Wilton Lions Club comes out on Sunday morning to set up pancake breakfasts where visitors are fed all they can eat at a modest price.

The bicycling season along the Elroy-Sparta State Trail runs from about May 1 to mid-October. This takes it through the season of brilliant fall color, which is always a popular natural show in that region.

Maintenance of the trail is excellent. After the track was removed, Wisconsin converted the railroad bed to a trail by laying down fine limestone screenings three to five inches deep, then packing them. A good rain quickly converts this to a hard biking surface. Railroad trestles were floored and railings were added for safety.

Many of the riders using this trail are Wisconsin people, but the state estimates that 55 per cent of the riders come from out of state. Chicago is an easy drive and thousands of Illinois people flock to Wisconsin for vacations.

Once this trail began to catch on, Wisconsin looked for other segments of old railroad that could be converted. One became the twenty-three-mile-long Sugar River Trail south of Madison, much like the Elroy-Sparta Trail in its development. Access to the trail on the east is at Brodhead. New Glarus, at the other end, lies in the heart of America's "Little Switzerland" region.

Up in Door County, in the thumb region of Wisconsin, there is also the Ahnappee State Trail, following fifteen miles of old railroad bed through picturesque countryside known for trout fishing, fruit orchards and Lake Michigan fishing villages. Southern access to the trail is on the northern edge of Algoma. The northern access is near Sturgeon Bay, where the trail intersects Nelson Road. There are numerous access points between. Another, the sixteen-mile-long Bearskin Trail, also on an abandoned railroad bed, runs between the village of Minocqua on the north and Highway K north of Haefford Junction on the south.

In addition, this bicycling state has mapped bike routes that cross the state in both general north-south and east-west directions. The Elroy-Sparta Trail, Wisconsin's most famous, is part of the three-hundred-mile-long Wisconsin Bikeway, which extends from Kenosha, on the shore of Lake Michigan north of Chicago, to La Crosse, a Mississippi River city on the other side of the state. This route is marked most of the way, well enough to enable bicyclists to follow it along a network of back roads that lead through scenic countryside and avoid heavy motor vehicle traffic.

Once you have reached La Crosse, if you still have steam enough, you can travel right onto the connecting North-South Wisconsin Bikeway and follow it for another three hundred and five miles.

If creation of this scenic route can be traced to a single person, the credit must go to Ellef Ellefson who, prior to his retirement, was a farmer and nurseryman; he is still a bicyclist. His experiences in seeing the bike route completed can serve as an example to other like-minded persons. Ellefson spread word within the American Youth Hostels organization about the general route to follow in making a tour north or south in Wisconsin. He also worked with planning commissions and communities until the route was eventually designated by the state and marked with signs. This led to publication of an excellent map and brochure describing the route. Free copies are available.

Wisconsin has been one of the leaders in developing highly useful maps especially for bicyclists. Trail maps are available at no cost from:

Department of Business Development
Wisconsin Bureau of Tourism
123 West Washington Avenue
Madison, WI 53703

One of the many popular bicycling areas in California and Nevada is found in the Lake Tahoe region, about one hundred miles east of Sacramento. Riders can take their bicycles aboard Amtrak and go to Truckee as a starting point. This is exciting bicycling country for those who are in top condition, but hills are steep and long. Remember the automobile traffic at all times, because this is always a busy region. Bright, easily seen clothes are important. Caltrans, California's Department of Transportation, offers a map of the area. Ask for "Lake Tahoe Bicycle Touring Guide."

California's longest bike trail was established as part of the 1976 Bicentennial celebration. Riders had long seen the possibility of designating a trail that would extend all the way from Oregon to Mexico, leading bicyclists through California's beautiful coastal country. Vacationers in this region can now follow a marked bicycle route, the "Pacific Coast Bicentennial Route," extending for a thousand miles down the California coast, with campgrounds and other facilities along the way.

This route offers a variety of surroundings and climate, ranging from mountains and forests in the northern part of the state to the hot, dry country in the south. There are beaches along the way and places where the trail leads through

Planners frequently route bicycle trails along harbors and through other scenic areas. SCHWINN BICYCLE COMPANY.

nearly level, irrigated valleys. And there are dozens of towns and cities with festivals and other seasonal activities.

Rainfall comes to California mostly from November into April, and ranges from seventy inches a year in the north to ten inches in the San Diego area. The Pacific Coast Bicentennial Route is generally ridden from north to south; riders can return by Amtrak. Most bicyclists using this route, however, do not travel the entire one thousand miles, but instead carve out sections of the route to fit their plans. If you want to ride the full route, you should be in top condition before starting and have a bicycle that is also in excellent shape. The full trip is likely to take the biggest part of a month.

Step one, if you're thinking of planning such a journey, is to order a copy of "Pacific Coast Bicycle Route" from Caltrans Publications Unit, 6002 Folsom Blvd., Sacramento, CA 95819. This is a spiral-bound, pocket-size booklet of strip maps that show the entire Oregon-to-Mexico route, complete with camping areas and other facilities. The price is $1.00, and California residents should add tax.

Remember that on this trip through California, or any trip in this highly populated state, you share the highways with heavy automobile traffic.

If a thousand miles of coastal riding in California is not enough, you can plan your trip to take you through Washington and Oregon as well. Information for these states is obtained from the Washington State Department of Highways, Olympia, WA 98504, and Oregon Department of Transportation, State Highway Building, Salem, OR 97310. Highway 101 along the whole coast of Oregon is a marked bike route and a highly scenic one. A folder, "Oregon Bike Routes," shows this route, plus others for the state, complete with details on facilities and information on grades. Oregon in recent times has become highly active in developing and maintaining bicycle routes. One per cent of the state's gasoline tax revenues go into this work, and state laws

New bicycle trails are being established every year all around the country. This 2.7-mile-long Alton Baker Park bikeway takes riders along the Willamette River in Eugene, Oregon, and is part of a much larger trail system. Part of Oregon's gasoline tax goes into constructing trails. OREGON DEPARTMENT OF TRANSPORTATION PHOTO.

require highway planners to consider bicyclists' needs.

Another state that has become a leader in designation of bicycle routes is Ohio. There is now a marked trail leading bicyclists completely across the state from west to east. It is marked for travel in either direction, a distance of 310 miles. This route, developed by the Columbus Council, American Youth Hostels, Inc., is known as the Cardinal Trail. The best information available for planning a trip or traveling on the Cardinal Trail is a pocket-size booklet of strip maps available from the Columbus Council A.Y.H., c/o Edward Honton, 1719 Eddystone Avenue, Columbus, OH 43224. The price is $3.50. If you want the plastic edition that will hold up under heavier use and wet weather, send $5.50.

Honton and the Columbus A.Y.H. Council have also published another book of Ohio bicycling maps, outlining thirty-six shorter circle routes through various sections of the state.

This bridge was built near the University of Oregon to enable bicyclists to cross the Willamette River. OREGON DEPARTMENT OF TRANSPORTATION PHOTO.

THE BIKE TRAILS ARE WAITING

COURTESY BIKECENTENNIAL.

Among the routes certain to become increasingly popular in Ohio is the trail built on forty-five miles of abandoned railroad along the scenic Little Miami River. This route winds down through the hills of southwestern Ohio into the eastern edge of Cincinnati.

Another good program is found in North Carolina. The state's Department of Transportation decided that there were many roads in North Carolina which, though relatively safe for bicycling, were not utilized by cyclists, largely because riders did not know about them. These routes were surveyed, then linked together in a network of bicycle routes. North Carolina then published a series of pamphlets designed especially for use by bicyclists. As the state proceeded with this plan, both federal workers and state workers in other states began to take notice and adopted parts of their procedure. When completed, this pioneering system will contain more than five thousand miles of bicycling routes. It is not surprising that other states have found methods worth copying in this plan. If you look, for example, at North Carolina's map of the 55-mile-long Sliding Rock bike route, you learn that, although the road is excellent, there are long grades and steep hills and you are told precisely where these are. You are also told that there are tunnels where you will need lights and informed about locations of camping areas and scenic attractions.

The East Coast Bike Trail, stretching more than seven hundred miles and going through several states, has its northern trailhead at the Boston Common. To ride this route you should be in good condition, even though it is not one of the country's most difficult trails. The first section, from Boston Common to Dudley, which is only three miles from Connecticut, is sixty miles. There is a hostel in Dudley, and along the route are motels and campgrounds.

The next section of one hundred and twenty miles leads through the Connecticut Valley with state parks, old villages and scenic farm country. Then comes the ninety-mile Hudson Valley segment, leading through the Catskill Mountains, which have plenty of motels as well as two hostels. The Delaware Water Gap section of the route leads through New Jersey for one hundred and twenty-five miles. Dairy farms and green fields predominate, but the Water Gap is a gorge that provides unforgettable scenery.

The next one-hundred-and-ten-mile stretch of the East Coast Bike Trail is through the Delaware Valley. Cyclists reach the C&D Canal after passing innumerable small towns, pedaling through Pennsylvania farming country and touring Valley Forge. Then comes the Chesapeake Bay section, leading for one hundred miles through little Eastern Shore towns and mostly flat rural countryside.

The fifty-mile-long route through the Potomac Valley extends from Patuxent to the Harry Nice Bridge. Then the Tidewater Virginia section extends for eighty miles of lightly traveled roads through farm areas and forested countryside.

For added information on the East Coast Bike Trail, contact East Coast Bicycle Congress, 333 East 25th Street, Baltimore, MD 21218.

Following its success in working out a route for the Trans-America Trail for the 1976 Bicentennial celebration, Bikecentennial began work on two other major trails. The first one finished was the Great Parks Trail, leading bicyclists from Jasper, in Alberta, Canada, south to Mesa Verde National Park in Colorado. This route leads cyclists through some of the world's most scenic country. The parks through which the trail passes include Jasper, Banff, Waterton Lakes and Kootenay in Canada; then, in the United States, Glacier, Yellowstone, Grand Tetons, Rocky Mountain National Park and, finally, Mesa Verde.

At one point, the route intersects the Trans-America Trail and follows it for several hundred miles, cutting off at Estes Park to go south to-

Special bicycle trails and bridges through park areas and forests give riders an opportunity to escape the competition of motor vehicles. U. S. DEPARTMENT OF TRANSPORTATION PHOTO, JAMES CARROLL.

ward Mesa Verde. Bikecentennial publishes maps of its trails and sells these out of its headquarters. Write Bikecentennial, P.O. Box 8308, Missoula, MT 59807.

Following completion of the Great Parks Trail, Bikecentennial concentrated on the Great Rivers Trail, designed to follow the course of the Mississippi from its headwaters in Minnesota to the Gulf of Mexico. This trail begins in Fargo, North Dakota, then swings up to Itaska State Park, where the big river actually begins. For hundreds of miles, bicyclists on the Great Rivers Trail ride down through the heart of America in a region famous for steamboats and Mark Twain.

Many states have shorter trails marked for bicyclists, often special loop trails leading to choice vacationing areas. Examples include Indiana's sixty-six-mile-long Whitewater Valley Route and sixty-two-mile-long Hoosier Hills Route. The Indiana Tourism Development Commission, 336 State House, Indianapolis, IN 46204, has maps. In South Dakota you can obtain a statewide Bicycle Riding Map from the Department of Tourism and Economic Development in Pierre.

Michigan's multitude of cyclists have available to them an outstanding set of maps. The Michigan plan was to ask experienced bicyclists in every one of the state's 83 counties to select and describe the best routes for bicycling. The chosen routes were marked in red on county maps. Then these maps were printed and boxed in a set of 48 individual sheets, printed on both sides. The boxed set can be obtained for $9.95 from Michigan Natural Resources Reference Library, Box 30034, Lansing, MI 48909.

The point is that, more than ever before, there are bicycle routes and good maps available, probably closer to you than you realize. Often all that is needed to open up new vistas is a letter to your own state capital, where the department of tourism, natural resources or transportation has bicycling information waiting.

MAP YOUR OWN TRAILS

Much of the bicycle mapping being done across the country is the product of amateur bicyclists, especially local bicycle clubs. If there is no bike route already explored through your region, creating a route could be an excellent club project or a good spare-time activity for a small group of cyclists, organized or not. The information must come from those who get out and ride. Creating a good bicycle route is not as simple as sitting behind a desk and making marks on an existing highway map.

The basic consideration is to devise a route that will be fun to ride and reasonably safe. One interesting idea is to create a bicycle trail around

A bicycling club tour gets underway on a quiet road in north Florida. FLORDIA NEWS BUREAU PHOTO.

a theme. The route might lead to historic homes in the area or to popular natural features including beaches, dunes, gorges, overlooks or wildlife sanctuaries.

Routes can usually be planned to bring riders back to a starting point and sometimes can include existing bicycle paths that are free of traffic.

The challenge is usually to select the best of several possible routes between various points. Narrowing the choice down depends on several factors, especially safety from heavy motor vehicle traffic. The quickest way to size up the alternatives is by automobile. Drive the possible routes, but watch with the eyes of a bicyclist for special hazards and potential difficulties. If possible, eliminate unpaved roads. You may be able to select roads with a pavement wide enough to include a paved strip outside the marked auto lane. How smooth is the road? Potholes are bicycling hazards, especially on downhill runs. Blind corners are also hazards, and so are storm-sewer grates with spaces that bike wheels can drop into.

Grades are important, and you may be able to plan the route so riders can go down the steepest hills instead of up them.

The acid test comes in bicycling the route. During this ride you will want to write down your observations. This is the beginning of a map. The more useful information you can include on the map, the better. There should be details on public picnic areas and parks, camping, towns and points of interest. Publishing the map, like plotting the route, makes a good club project.

County maps are helpful in locating the less-heavily-used roads and often include paved roads that are not even on state highway maps.

Bicycle clubs in neighboring communities can combine their efforts and link their favorite trails into longer routes if they coordinate their efforts. They can also be influential in getting official help to have the bicycle route recognized and posted with signs.

11.
BICYCLES IN THE NATIONAL PARKS

Whether they are bicyclists or not, Americans who think of touring almost automatically include the national parks in their plans. This is understandable, because our country has perhaps the world's finest system of national parks. Some are better suited to bicycling than others, but even the mountainous parks are toured by experienced bicyclists in good physical condition.

The National Park Service, part of the Department of the Interior, is responsible for nearly 300 areas across the entire country, not all of which are called national parks. Some are national monuments, national recreation areas, national historic sites, national lakeshores or national parkways.

According to the Code of Federal Regulations, bicycling is permitted on public roads throughout the National Park system. Some park areas have special trails for bicycling; rangers in any park you enter will know about them. The Code of Federal Regulations requires riders in all the national park areas to obey traffic rules, keep well to the side of the road, ride in single file unless on roads designated "bicycles only" and have lights on bikes at night or during periods of low visibility. Riders may encounter special cases prohibiting the riding of bicycles in some park areas; where this is the case, there will be signs posted or maps will be marked giving the details on when and where such restrictions apply. This can be determined in advance by writing to the superintendent of the park you plan to visit.

No two of these park areas are alike. There are a wide variety of landscapes in the national parks, and this is part of their appeal. Here is a sampling of national park areas that are special favorites with bicycling tourists.

EVERGLADES

Throughout the National Park system there is probably no better place for bicycle touring than the Everglades National Park in southern Florida. Although winds are sometimes a problem, the incredibly flat terrain more than compensates for this.

The Everglades is a river, 50 miles wide and inches deep. Out of its shimmering waters, making their way sluggishly toward the sea, grow broad fields of sawgrass stretching away to the horizon. Within this "sea of grass" stand little islands, slightly higher, and covered with tangles of bushes and trees. These islands are the homes of alligators, bobcats, otter, deer, bears and a multitude of long-legged wading birds.

Much of the fun of visiting the Everglades is looking for the wildlife. If you carry a camera, this is the place to use it. There are few better places anywhere to photograph wading birds on a winter or spring morning than the ponds along the highway that runs out to Flamingo. About daybreak these ponds are often crowded with herons, egrets, pelicans, storks, ducks and roseate spoonbills. These birds feed in the shallows, pay-

Touring bicyclists should take the time to enjoy their trip. These riders are bird-watching in the Everglades National Park, Florida. PHOTO BY THE AUTHOR.

ing little attention to photographers on the nearby shore. In addition, there are alligators in the ponds and along the ditches and you may even spot a bobcat crossing the road ahead of you.

Winter is the best season for visiting the Everglades. The north is still locked in so much ice and snow that enjoyable bicycle riding is impossible through much of the country. But this vast subtropical region of Florida is warm and sunny. In this season the mosquitoes are seldom a problem. In addition, the nonresident wild birds are down from the north and birds are concentrated in feeding areas. Summer, on the other hand, brings hot weather and mosquitoes.

Park naturalists conduct a continuing series of programs for Everglades visitors, ranging from slide presentations to hikes on which you slosh through the swamp. Details on these programs are posted at visitors' headquarters and campgrounds.

Rental bicycles, including tandems, are available at the visitor center in Flamingo, though many visitors bring their own bicycles. Experienced bicycle tourists should consider flying, with their bicycles, into the Miami International Airport, then pedaling from there out to the park. You can overnight in Homestead, which is slightly more than fifty miles from Flamingo. At park headquarters, pick up a copy of the map of the Everglades Bicycle Path. This trail, beginning at Royal Palms Visitor Center, includes some seldom-traveled, and sometimes unpaved, service roads that lead to areas and camping locations that you cannot reach by automobile.

As you travel the thirty-eight miles of paved park roads out to Flamingo, which was once an isolated fishing village, take time for the special trails and side trips. The number of roads in the park is limited and getting lost is seldom a problem. Even if you normally tour at a fast pace, you will want to allow extra time in the Everglades. There are many places in the world where you can ride fast, but no other place anywhere that you can tour a region like the Everglades.

There is a motel at Flamingo, but there are also fine campgrounds throughout the area.

Vacationers often find rental bicycles available at their favorite destinations. These bicycles are rented at Cade's Cove Campground, Great Smoky Mountains National Park, Tennessee. NATIONAL PARK SERVICE PHOTO, FRED R. BELL.

Flamingo itself is an excellent place to stay for a few days while you explore. If you belong to the League of American Wheelmen, you can plan your Everglades visit to coincide with its annual Winter Rendezvous at Homestead and join others for a trip into the park.

THE BLUE RIDGE

Some bicyclists like the hill-country riding they find on the Blue Ridge Parkway. This special road, managed by the National Park Service, runs from Shenandoah National Park in northern Virginia to the Great Smoky Mountains National Park on the border of Tennessee and North Carolina. For 469 miles the Parkway follows high ridges, giving travelers sweeping views of the ancient, haze-shrouded Appalachian Mountains. Elevations along the Parkway range from 649 to 6,053 feet.

This is cool and colorful country where, from mid-May to mid-June, the highway is lined with brilliant displays of wild azalea and rhododendron. Little farms with split-rail fences appear occasionally beside the Parkway. There are campgrounds along the road, although these were spaced with automobile tourists in mind. There are also stores where you can stock up on supplies.

The Blue Ridge Parkway is a two-lane highway which commercial traffic cannot use. There are no trucks to blow you off the road. Vehicles are all expected to travel at modest speeds. But this is tourist country and the grades were designed for automobiles. Bicycles are permitted the length of the Parkway, but this is a ride for the experienced bicyclist in good physical condition.

There are a number of ways for bicyclists to see the Blue Ridge Parkway. One would be to ride the entire 469 miles and perhaps include the connecting 105-mile Skyline Drive in the Shenandoah National Park, traveling either with or without a sag wagon. The Skyline Drive has one 700-foot tunnel near Thornton Gap, requiring lights. Or you might plan a trip for any segment of the Parkway. If you normally transport your bicycle on car racks, you can plan a series of stays at the various campgrounds along the Parkway, then make daily trips out and back from each campground, first in one direction, then the other, changing camps every couple of days.

Remember that you will need lights if you travel any of the Parkway tunnels. Also, bicycling is limited to daylight hours and, whether you like it or not, bicyclists must yield the right of way to motor vehicles.

NATCHEZ TRACE

Another parkway considered an outstanding bicycle touring trail is the famous Natchez Trace. This historic 450-mile-long route was traveled in the early 1800s by river boatmen from Ken-

Among the favorite bicycling routes in the National Park Service areas is the Natchez Trace Parkway, with hundreds of miles of uncongested, gently rolling to level terrain. NATIONAL PARK SERVICE PHOTO, JOHN MOHLHENRITH.

tucky. These flatboaters floated their loads of furs and other goods down the Mississippi to New Orleans, then sold the logs in their boats as well as the goods they carried and made their way home on foot. The woodland trail they followed was previously used by Indians, and before that by wild game.

Today the National Park Service maintains the trail for travelers who like to journey through the pleasant countryside of Tennessee, Alabama and Mississippi. Spring and autumn are especially comfortable along the Trace, while summer tends to be hot and humid. In villages and at crossroads near the Trace there are motels and service stations.

Among the attractions that draw bicyclists to this route are the lack of commercial traffic (trucks are forbidden) and the reasonable speed limit for motor vehicles. The road is smooth and pleasant for bicycling. You should consider the prevailing winds in determining the direction of travel. Generally the north-to-south trip is the choice if you are riding the Trace in only one direction. You can then return by bus from Natchez, or by air, bringing your bicycle along as baggage. A few sections of the Trace are not yet completed, but there are easily negotiated connecting roads.

The three campgrounds on the Trace are spaced to accommodate motor vehicle travelers more than bicycling tourists, but there are also other camping areas, including state parks. The National Park Service publishes a leaflet on the Natchez Trace.

C&O CANAL

Bicyclists in the East travel the Chesapeake and Ohio Canal National Park, whose 184-mile-long trail begins at Washington, D.C. Canal boats here transported flour, wood, grain and coal before the railroads came into prominence. Boats were towed along the canals by teams of mules walking the banks. It is their tow paths that eventually became today's bicycle trail. The trail, about eight feet wide, is hard-packed dirt. Much of the time it leads beneath overhanging trees that shade the path. Water still flows through the canal, and canoeists paddle the slack-water pools and portage around the locks.

Along this trail, cyclists will find camping areas every five miles or so for the 162 miles between Seneca and Cumberland. First come, first served. Almost all of these campsites are reached by hiking or biking in, and not by automobile. There are many nearby villages for picking up supplies. The best way to tour this route is to plan an easy thirty miles or so a day, leaving time to relax and explore along the route.

ACADIA

If your travels take you to Maine and Acadia National Park, by all means take your bike along. This vacationland in the northeastern corner of the country is a national park unlike any other, and the bicycle is a good way of getting around, as a growing number of visitors are discovering.

Acadia, whose black, rocky shores are battered by the Atlantic, is rugged territory. Here you watch the changing moods of the sea. Accompanying a Park Service naturalist, you may encounter porpoises, seals, ospreys and eagles. Or you may visit a nesting colony of sea birds.

Some roads in the park are one-way, and bicyclists must go with the traffic. The park supplies riders with a map outlining three scenic bicycle trips.

CAPE HATTERAS

Cape Hatteras National Seashore would seem a natural for bicycling. There are shipwrecks, long sandy beaches, seabirds, excellent fishing and beach camping. But competition with automobiles is heavy enough to discourage some bicyclists. If you can buck the traffic, take your bike along and ride Highway 12 to sand dunes, little fishing villages, a lighthouse, a wildlife refuge and camping with the sound of the surf for background music.

CAPE COD

Another National Seashore managed by the National Park Service and well known to bicyclists is on Cape Cod, that sickle-shaped arm of Massachusetts, famous as the first landing place of the Pilgrims. The three short bicycle trails within the National Seashore are paved, and no motorized vehicles, Mopeds included, are allowed on them.

The National Park Service provides maps of the bicycle trails within Cape Cod National Seashore; these can be picked up as you come into the area. One of the trails, a gentle two-mile ride in the North Truro area, is known as the Head of Meadow Trail and holds special interest for its historic significance. Flanked by sand dunes and Salt Meadow, this trail follows part of the Old Kings Highway, which was the first road to Provincetown.

For more sand dunes, ponds and woods there is the eight-mile-long Province Lands Trail near Provincetown. This one is somewhat more challenging, with its steep grades and sharp curves.

Cape Cod is fine bicycling country without difficult hills. Towns there are catering to the growing number of bicyclists. Some are turning old railroad rights-of-way into bike trails, and bicycle rental agencies are proliferating on the Cape. Beaches and other public areas are equipped with racks for parking.

Obtain a copy of the *Massachusetts Bicycle Atlas,* which gives details on numerous bicycle routes, especially in the eastern section of the Bay State. These routes are the work of the volunteer Trails Advisory Committee, working with the State Department of Natural Resources. The pioneering work of exploring and camping these trails was carried out by the Charles River Wheelmen, a Cambridge-based bicycle club affiliated with the League of American Wheelmen. The *Bicycle Atlas* is available from the Massachusetts Department of Fisheries, Wildlife and Recreational Vehicles, 100 Cambridge St., Boston, MA 02202.

GREAT SMOKIES

Only the most rugged bicyclists might think of the Great Smoky Mountains National Park as suitable for bicycling, but a growing number of riders are finding this an interesting and challenging place to pedal. The choice section is a valley the settlers called Cades Cove. Here, early farmers of the region built their log homes and a mill, and seldom ventured beyond their isolated hill community. The Park Service maintains some of the original structures to give visitors a feeling of what life in Cades Cove was like a century ago. There is a narrow, one-way, eleven-mile-long paved road around Cades Cove.

Some bicyclists who are in shape for it and want the experience even pedal to the top of Clingman's Dome. The roads to the mountaintop are steep and crooked. From there you can look out across miles of slopes set in a gray-blue haze. To this day these mixed deciduous forests are the stronghold of bears, wild turkeys, grouse and

Bicycles are a favorite way to get around Cape Cod. NATIONAL PARK SERVICE PHOTO.

deer. Other roads lead along rushing streams with excellent trout fishing.

There are a number of campgrounds in the Great Smoky Mountains National Park. Midsummer is the busiest season—and the Great Smokies draw more visitors annually than any other national park in the country. Autumn, with its brilliant colors, is a splendid season in spite of the cool weather. And, with the children back in school, the big summer crowds are gone.

YELLOWSTONE

Yellowstone, oldest of our national parks and also the largest in the forty-eight contiguous states, is a wonderland whether you travel by bike, by car or on foot. Early mountain men who explored the Yellowstone told unbelievable stories of rivers that ran hot and cold, mud bubbling from the earth and geysers shooting steam far into the air. These reports were considered tall tales until others found that the stories about this northwestern corner of Wyoming were really true.

A bicycle tour through Yellowstone can be combined with a visit to the Grand Teton National Park. These neighboring parks are linked by a scenic highway leading through timbered mountains and flanked by snow-capped peaks. Here live bears, deer, elk and moose. Ospreys nest in craggy trees along the edges of the lakes, and beaver build their remarkable dams across the streams that wind through alpine meadows. There simply are few areas anywhere with the wealth of scenery that you encounter in this section of the Rocky Mountains.

Scenery aside, however, the bicyclist should understand the hazards of travel through these national parks. The biggest hazard of all, as in most places, is the automobile. There is always the tourist in a hurry to "do" two or three national parks a day, and anything slowing him down is seen as an obstacle. Yellowstone has especially heavy traffic during July and August. A good time to be in this park, as in many others, is just before school is dismissed in the spring or after it resumes in fall.

Bicyclists, however, travel the park roads right through the summer months and for the most part have no serious problems with traffic. In many instances, though, the campgrounds are spaced too far apart to accommodate bicyclists comfortably. In addition, they are filled on a

Scenic western roads are drawing growing numbers of bicyclists. These cyclists are passing the 12,605-foot Mt. Moran in Grand Teton National Park. WYOMING TRAVEL COMMISSION PHOTO.

Tourists who travel by bicycle should leave time enough in their schedules to stop beside a mountain lake or stream. WYOMING TRAVEL COMMISSION PHOTO.

Yosemite's scenic valley provides an unforgettable bicycling experience. NATIONAL PARK SERVICE PHOTO

These visitors to the nation's capital are bicycling on a trail near the John F. Kennedy Center. NATIONAL PARK SERVICE PHOTO, JACK ROTTIER.

first-come, first-served basis, which can mean "No Vacancy" signs by midafternoon, when cyclists are still miles up the road, pedaling. In a few campgrounds, because of the bear threat, campers may be limited to sleeping in vehicles. By reserving in advance, however, visitors can arrange indoor accommodations through the concessionaires within the park.

Grand Teton National Park is generally somewhat less crowded. Any touring schedule here should allow you time to enjoy some of the extra attractions. While in the Grand Tetons, arrange a float trip on the Snake River and watch for the nesting bald eagles. Keep your camera handy because you will want to look at the color pictures of this scenic land for years to come.

YOSEMITE

As John Muir said of Yosemite, "None can escape its charm." Within this national park, lying east of San Francisco, there are spectacular granite cliffs, peaks, domes and hanging valleys with giant waterfalls. There are also spectacular tall sequoia trees, alpine meadows and uncounted wild creatures. The park covers 1,189 square miles.

Within this unforgettable park are two hundred miles of scenic roads where commercial trucks are limited to local traffic and motorists are required to drive at reasonable speeds, for the most part, a maximum of 35 miles per hour. No wonder this is a favorite place for bicyclists. There are also bicycle trails where no motor vehicles are permitted.

Bicyclists have the advantage that, if they want to stop to take a picture, they may do so, while motorists must find an authorized parking place. Within Yosemite Valley, roads are mostly flat.

REDWOOD COUNTRY

If your vacation travels take you to northern California, consider bicycling through the stronghold of the giant redwoods. No place else on earth will you find such impressive trees—the world's tallest plants, and some of the oldest. Standing beneath a giant redwood is a humbling experience, and bicycling along the shaded avenues through these groves is a magnificent ride.

For forty miles between Crescent City and Orick, U. S. Highway 101—which is part of the Pacific Coast Bikecentennial Route—runs through Redwoods National Park. Freeway shoulders along this section of U.S. 101 are open to bicyclists. There are some steep grades here, and weather can be wet and windy, especially during the months from November to March, but spring and fall bring weather that is clear, cool and pleasant. Summer mornings are often foggy, but if this is less than perfect for the bicyclist, it is just right for the redwoods—fog is one of the reasons they are growing where they are.

Camping here is in state park campgrounds. There are walk-in campsites that can be used by bicyclists, at fees considerably lower than those charged in the campsites built for motorists.

This park, as with most national parks, is best appreciated by those who take time to slow down and look around them, including up into the tops of those skyscraper trees.

There are other national parks suited to bicycling, and you will discover them from coast to coast in your travels. Chances are excellent that in the coming years touring bicyclists are going to ride the roads of the national parks more than they ever have before—and in the process get a better view of their unique and beautiful features than they could if they traveled in motor vehicles.

NATIONAL PARK SYSTEM AREAS CONTAINING BICYCLE TRAILS

PARK	NUMBER OF BICYCLE TRAILS	TRAIL MILEAGE
Acadia National Park, Maine	1	15
Cape Cod National Seashore, Massachusetts	3	12
Chesapeake & Ohio Canal National Historical Park, Maryland	1	184
Rock Creek Park, D.C.	2	9
George Washington Memorial Pkwy, Va.-D.C.	1	16
Potomac Parks, Ellipse and Mall, D.C.	4	12
Fort Circle-Anacostia, D.C.	1	12
Everglades National Park, Florida	2	24
Scotts Bluff National Monument, Nebraska	1	1
Indiana Dunes National Lakeshore, Ind. Calumet Bike Trail	1	9
Chickasaw National Recreation Area, Oklahoma	1	4
Pea Ridge National Military Park, Arkansas	1	7
Glacier National Park	1	2
Yosemite National Park, California	1	10
Point Reyes National Seashore, California	4	17
Hawaii Volcanoes National Park, Hawaii	1	5
TOTALS	26	339

NATIONAL PARK SERVICE

For information on these National Park Service areas of special interest to bicycle tourists, write to the Superintendent at the following addresses:

Acadia National Park, R 1, Box 1, Bar Harbor, ME 04609

Assateague Island National Seashore, R 2, Box 294, Berlin, MD 21811

Badlands National Monument, P.O. Box 6, Interior, SD 57750

Blue Ridge Parkway, 700 Northwestern Bank Bldg., Asheville, NC 28801

Canyonlands National Park, 446 S. Main St., Moab, UT 84532

Cape Cod National Seashore, South Wellfleet, MA 02663.

Cape Hatteras National Seashore, R 1, Box 675, Manteo, NC 27954

Carlsbad Caverns National Park, 3225 National Parks Hwy., Carlsbad, NM 88220

Chesapeake & Ohio Canal National Historical Park, Box 158, Sharpsburg, MD 21782

Death Valley National Monument, Death Valley, CA 92328

Delaware Water Gap National Recreation Area, Bushkill, PA 18324

Everglades National Park, P.O. Box 279, Homestead, FL 33030

Fire Island National Seashore, 120 Laurel St., Patchogue, NY 11772

Grand Canyon National Park, P.O. Box 129, Grand Canyon, AZ 86023

Grand Teton National Park, P.O. Box 67, Moose, WY 83012

Great Smoky Mountains National Park, Gatlinburg, TN 37738

Hawaii Volcanoes National Park, Hawaii National Park, HI 96718

Indiana Dunes National Lakeshore, R 2, Box 139A, Chesterton, IN 46304

Joshua Tree National Monument, 74485 Palm Vista Dr., Twentynine Palms, CA 92277

Lake Mead National Recreation Area, 601 Nevada Hwy., Boulder City, NV 89005

Mammoth Cave National Park, Mammoth Cave, KY 42259

Natchez Trace Parkway, R 1, NT-142, Tupelo, MS 38801

National Capital Parks, 1100 Ohio Dr. S.W., Washington, DC 20242

Organ Pipe Cactus National Monument, P.O. Box 38, Ajo, AZ 85321

Petrified Forest National Park, AZ 86028

Point Reyes National Seashore, Point Reyes, CA 94956

Redwood National Park, Drawer N, Crescent City, CA 95531

Saguaro National Monument, P.O. Box 17210, Tucson, AZ 85731

Shenandoah National Park, R 4, Box 292, Luray, VA 22836

Theodore Roosevelt National Memorial Park, Medora, ND 58645

Wind Cave National Park, Hot Springs, SD 57747

Yellowstone National Park, P.O. Box 168, WY 82190

Yosemite National Park, P.O. Box 577, CA 95389

For detailed information on the national parks in any part of the country, write the National Park Service in the following regional offices:

North Atlantic, 15 State St., Boston, MA 20109
(Maine, New Hampshire, Connecticut, Rhode Island, Vermont, Massachusetts, New York, New Jersey)

Mid-Atlantic, 143 S. Third St., Philadelphia, PA 19106
(Pennsylvania, Maryland, West Virginia, Delaware, Virginia)

National Capital, 1100 Ohio Dr., S.W., Washington, DC 20243
(District of Columbia, parts of Maryland, Virginia, West Virginia)

Southeast, 1895 Phoenix Blvd., Atlanta, GA 30349
(Kentucky, Tennessee, North Carolina, South Carolina, Mississippi, Alabama, Georgia, Florida, Puerto Rico, Virgin Islands)

Midwest, 1970 Jackson St., Omaha, NE 68102
(Ohio, Indiana, Michigan, Wisconsin, Illinois, Minnesota, Iowa, Missouri, Nebraska, Kansas)

Rocky Mountain, P.O. Box 25287, Denver, CO 80225
(Montana, North Dakota, South Dakota, Wyoming, Utah, Colorado)

Southwest, P.O. Box 728, Santa Fe, NM 87501
(Arkansas, Louisiana, Texas, Oklahoma, New Mexico, part of Arizona)

Western, Box 36063, 450 Golden Gate Ave., San Francisco, CA 94102
(California, Nevada, most of Arizona, Hawaii)

Pacific Northwest, Fourth and Pike Bldg., Rm. 927, 1424 Fourth Avenue, Seattle, WA 98101
(Idaho, Oregon, Washington, Alaska)

12.

THE TOURING CYCLIST

As owning and riding a bicycle begins to grow on you, there comes the temptation to use your two-wheeler to see the country on longer trips. Some riders set off alone and go where the days lead them. Others prefer to travel with company, either one other cyclist, or a small group of compatible travelers who know in advance that they can get along well together. Strong arguments in favor of traveling with at least one companion include the fact that experiences shared are more fun. Besides, when people bicycle together, there is help available if a machine breaks down or a rider becomes ill or injured.

Bicycle tours may be anything from a few hours to months in length. Before leaping onto a new bike and setting off across the continent, plan to build up your experience and physical condition with a series of shorter trips. Gradually, you gain confidence in yourself and your bike as you learn to shift gears smoothly, take the hills and deal with traffic. Shorter trips condition your body physically and your mind psychologically for longer tours.

THE ONE-DAY TOUR

A bicycle trip for one day should be planned just as carefully as a longer adventure is. You want the trip to be fun. It should lead you to points of interest and away from the features you want to escape. Plan it well, using such maps as you can round up. Pick routes leading through parks and open countryside where possible, along rivers or into the hills and farm country. Interesting, relaxing routes help you return in the evening refreshed and eager to go again.

Plan a circle tour, unless you can arrange to rendezvous with someone who will haul you and your bike back at the day's end. The circle tour gives you new scenery throughout the trip. Even if you are familiar with the route, the countryside will look different from a bicycle.

Consider the prevailing winds. If you live in an area where mornings are normally still but the wind comes up in the afternoon, ride your circle tour in the direction that promises to put the wind at your back during the last part of the trip.

THE TOURING CYCLIST

By equipping saddle or handlebars with small bags in which they carry lunch, rain equipment and a basic tool kit, riders are ready for daylong tours. Inexperienced riders in mountainous terrain usually find twenty miles of riding enough for the day. SCHWINN BICYCLE COMPANY.

These daylong trips can be given an added purpose if you are a photographer, fisherman, artist or bird watcher. The equipment needed for any of these interests can be easily taken along on the bike.

You need not weigh down your bike with loaded panniers and heavy packs for these short trips. The few items you need can be fitted into a single pack on the bike rack behind the saddle or into a handlebar pack. Take along drinking water, a pump, a tool kit, a tire repair kit and rain gear.

LONGER TRIPS

For trips longer than one day, the additional equipment needed will primarily depend on your plans for eating and sleeping. Even if you plan to eat every meal in a restaurant, there is always the possibility of a breakdown or other emergency that could keep you from reaching a meal stop. Carry along lightweight food items for such emergencies. Other food should be packed for snacks. Emergency food is an especially sound idea when bicycling through the West. There are stretches of highway where you might not find a crossroads store—or water—for sixty miles or more.

Day-tripper bag fits back carrier. COURTESY HARTLEY ALLEY, THE TOURING CYCLIST SHOP.

Rations you carry need not be elaborate nor add much weight to your pack. Nuts, raisins, dried fruit, processed cheese from the supermarket and candy bars that you can buy from a camping or wilderness supply store will provide high energy in relation to their weight.

If you intend to reach a motel at the end of every day, planning is especially important, right down to advance reservations where possible.

LOADING UP
FOR THE TOUR

Anyone who travels by bicycle needs to give some serious thought to how all the necessary equipment can be packed into the available space. If you're putting a big suitcase into the trunk of a car, no problem. But if you are bicycle touring, you should take along a minimum number of essentials that can be packed in minimum space.

Most of us, at this point, lay the equipment out on the floor. Now we can take stock and check off items against the list to see that we have everything we need. Chances are that we also have a few items that will prove to be nonessentials. This business of packing has to be fitted to the individual traveler's needs and habits, and it is unlikely that any two of us will follow the same plan. But there are some general guidelines that can help.

Years ago, when I was off on a canoeing trip in the Quetico-Superior country, the guide told us in the beginning that the secret of getting across the portages with a minimum of fuss is not to carry a lot of small items. Instead, consolidate. This also applies to packing for a bicycle tour. Not only will you want to put all food items in the same place every day, but you will also find it helpful to pack the food in daily allotments, according to a meal plan worked out in advance. The best way to carry these items in your packs is to put them into individual see-through plastic bags. Plastic bags are fine organizers and they also protect your things from dust, dirt and moisture. Even clothes can be rolled and packed into bags.

Using these smaller bags also allows you to eliminate some packing materials. If you are carrying several rolls of film and keeping the 35 mm canisters in their cartons, you are wasting space. I take the round canisters out of the cartons and put them together in a plastic bag that can be sealed. To eliminate any question about what kind of film it is, I mark each canister with a grease pencil. The same principle can be applied to other items. The film, incidentally, should be kept cool. You can wrap film in an insulating layer of newspaper and pack it among your clothes.

How you pack, as well as what you take along, will vary depending on whether you are traveling with other bicyclists. There is no point in duplicating all the items. If you are likely to be close together throughout the trip, you will not all need a large crescent wrench. Campers traveling together can divide up the equipment by weight, bulk and ability of the riders.

PACKS
FOR THE BICYCLE

Even if you trim your equipment to the absolute minimum, you are going to need panniers on the back and probably a handlebar bag. You may find, as many beginning bicycle touring riders have, that before you are many days on the road you are trimming your load drastically to give you more freedom.

The rear panniers will require a rack over the back wheel. Select a carrier that fits rigidly and will give good wheel clearance with panniers attached. Check the models available (see Chapter 5) and select the one that fits the bicycle you will be riding. The carrier must allow clearance for center-pull caliper brakes if your machine is so equipped.

Select with care the bags you will hang from your bicycle. They should be rugged in construction, as weatherproof as you can get them, lightweight and designed to hold the maximum load for the space available. Those made with a number of smaller pockets are worth considering, because these provide places to carry camera equipment, snacks, suntan lotion or other frequently used items. You also want the packs to close securely and stay closed while you are riding. They should attach to the carriers or handlebars firmly so they don't slip or flop around. Baggage that keeps sliding out of position can take away much of the pleasure of touring.

When selecting panniers or handlebar bags, it is a good idea to actually fit them to your bicycle. See that the attachments for holding them are rugged and will keep them secure. If possible, the best plan is to actually load the kind of bags in which you are interested, then ride with them to see how the outfit feels.

The traveler off on a first tour is inclined to

THE TOURING CYCLIST

Trail pannier bag. Two zippered compartments and two "piggyback" compartments. All four are weather-flapped. Bag has four buckles for tie-down to carrier and stiffening boards for frame control. BISHOP FREEMAN COMPANY.

Rear panniers. COURTESY HARTLEY ALLEY, THE TOURING CYCLIST SHOP.

G/T Elite Panniers for fully equipped touring. HINE/SNOWBRIDGE, INC.

Day and night tripper. Stiffeners prevent bag from touching spokes or derailleur. Compartments are weather-flapped. Bag has five compartments plus top loops for tie-down of extras. BISHOP FREEMAN COMPANY.

load up the bicycle until it resembles a prospector's burro. With packs front and back, with items dangling and slipping, the whole adventure looks hopeless—and may be. The premium is on knowing how to travel light without forgetting essentials.

The handlebar bag adds weight to the front, but space in it can be saved for the lightweight items you might need along the way, such as food, a cap, suntan lotion, maps, a compass, a nylon jacket, sunglasses.

The best design for a handlebar bag is one in which the top cover opens on the side next to the handlebars. This enables the rider to get at the contents easily without dismounting. However, most handlebar bags are designed to open the other way. Some are equipped with a map compartment on the top, arranged so the map can be placed flat, in plain view through a clear plastic cover. The handlebar bag should be compact and should hold its shape in travel.

Panniers should be made to keep the weight low on the machine, for easier riding. Weight packed high adds to the instability of the bicycle. This applies to both front and back loads. When loading the pack, store the heavier items low in the pack for the same reason. If you are carrying a camp stove, pack it upright. Liquid fuel should also be kept upright to prevent leaking.

Check also the ease with which the bags can be fitted to the bicycle and removed. Some panniers can be fastened together when they are off the bike, for easy carrying by hand, or can be attached to a backpack.

In addition to panniers and a handlebar pack, you can add a small bag behind the saddle for tools or other equipment. Rugged lightweight stuff sacks, in which you can carry a sleeping bag or clothing, strapped directly to the carrier behind the seat, are also useful. Contents of the saddlebags and handlebar pack can be kept neat and more easily located if they are stored in individual bags. If these are plastic bags, they will keep items dry if the outer bags should prove to be less than waterproof. Seams on new bicycle bags and packs should be treated with a sealer to help shut out water.

Some riders try touring with a backpack or day pack on their backs. This is likely to be given up after a brief and probably not very comfortable trial run. The body should be kept as free as possible of weight and restrictive straps while pedaling. The one situation where you might want to make use of such a pack is on those short runs where you are bringing in groceries or water to your campsite from a nearby source.

Utility tool bag with zipper on three sides, reinforced top and stiffened bottom. BISHOP FREEMAN COMPANY.

Saddle Pak. Self-sealing zipper with nylon flap to prevent water entry. Cylinder shaped, 8½" long, 5" diameter. BISHOP FREEMAN COMPANY.

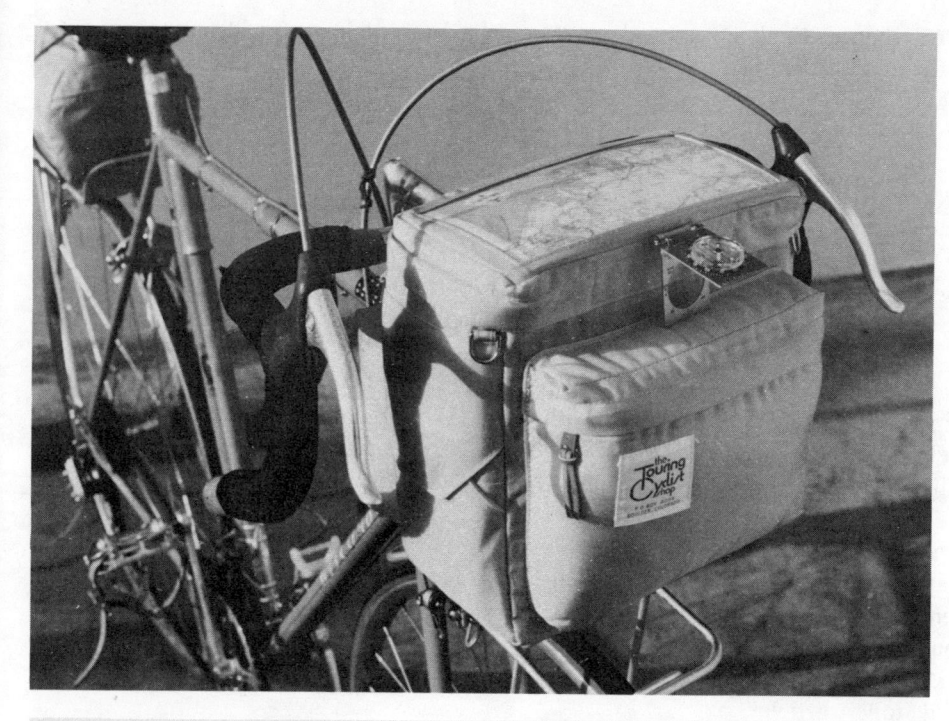

Handlebar bag with map carrier and loop for mounting Silva Huntsman compass. COURTESY HARTLEY ALLEY, THE TOURING CYCLIST SHOP.

Touring bicycle fully equipped with rear panniers, day tripper, handlebar bag and front panniers. COURTESY HARTLEY ALLEY, THE TOURING CYCLIST SHOP.

TRIMMING WEIGHT

Bicyclists, like backpackers, should think in terms of ounces as they put their packs together. The importance of this becomes especially evident after a day of pedaling against the wind or up a mountain.

The more self-sufficient you expect to be on the trip, the more equipment you must carry. If you stay at motels and eat at roadside restaurants, you eliminate sleeping bag, shelter, cooking equipment, and most food—and trim the pack by many pounds. But many touring bicyclists camp to minimize expenses. In either case, the rider can usually trim weight off the pack.

Begin by working out a checklist of items to take along and trim the list of nonessentials mercilessly. Then, shop for the smallest containers you can find of essential items. One can obviously go too far in leaving things behind. You will learn from experience and adjust your ideas of what is needed as you go along.

Here are some specifics for trimming weight. A strong plastic bag will hold toilet articles as safely as a heavier leather or plastic kit. Buy toothpaste in small tubes. Razors are available in extremely light weights, with long-lasting, double-edged steel blades. Leave the electric shaver home. Settle for the smallest can of shaving soap or, better yet, use face soap. Liquid soap can be carried in a plastic tube, available from camping supply stores, and this soap can be used for dishes, clothes and you—shaving included.

Be especially choosy about your clothes. Look for really lightweight items that will give maximum comfort for the kind of country you will travel through. A thin nylon windbreaker is important and adds only ounces. The poncho should be tough, but also light in weight.

Whatever you take, keep in mind that your body has to supply the energy to move the outfit, and that ounces add up rapidly. If you are camping along the way, your pack is probably going to add at least thirty pounds to your burden. If you are touring but not camping, you will still transport twenty or more pounds in addition to the weight of your bike. Water and special items such as your camera add to the weight drastically. I would think long and hard, however, before leaving the camera at home. You will want pictures of the trip later.

THE HOSTELING WAY

If you travel far by bicycle, you will meet people who build their trips around facilities offered by American Youth Hostels, Inc. Youth Hostels is a worldwide organization with headquarters in England and facilities in 61 countries. The purpose of the organization is to help people plan pleasant, low-cost trips.

There is no top age limit on membership, and older cyclists pedal into the hostels frequently. Half of the members are older than eighteen.

American Youth Hostels, Inc., sells a low-cost, cotton sleeping sack which you can carry away with you. The organization also sells its *North American Bicycle Atlas* at a modest price. It is an excellent book for anyone planning a bicycle tour.

For more information on this program write: American Youth Hostels, 132 Spring Street, New York, NY 10012.

BE A HOST

While he was touring in Europe, John Mosley was impressed with the fact that he could frequently stay in private homes. Why wasn't this done more extensively in his own country? Mosley thought it could be, so he created a plan based on his idea and made it a reality by starting an annually updated list of people—hundreds of them, in almost every state—who are willing to invite touring cyclists into their homes.

Plan participants, John says, do not include people who just want to find free accommodations. They are all cyclists who are willing to share their homes. "It is not a list of free lunches," says John, "nor is it something that people receive just for the asking. In general, the only way to get a copy [of the list] is to volunteer your own home on a reciprocal basis."

He calls his listing the "Touring Cyclists Hospitality Directory." People whose names and addresses are on the list offer a place to sleep and a shower to cyclists who contact them in advance. If you want to be included in the directory as a host and receive the list for planning your own travels, write to John Mosley, 13623 Sylvan, Van Nuys, CA 91401.

Bicyclists, more than motorists, see the world around them and have time to enjoy what they find along the trails. BICYCLE MANUFACTURERS ASSOCIATION OF AMERICA, INC., PHOTO.

PACE YOURSELF

Regardless of how you plan to live along the route, allow yourself time to relax. The tour should not be a highly regimented outing where you schedule yourself to reach point "A" by 2 P.M. and Point "B" at 4:35. Better to have a general plan, plus an overall "what the hell" attitude about your schedule, if indeed you have a schedule. When you come to a national park you especially like, a mountain deserving a photograph, or a trout stream that needs another day of fishing, stop or stay over. If you must be back on a given day, it is better to plan a shorter trip than to be forced to ride so hard you cannot slow down and enjoy.

USING MAPS

The most readily available maps are published by state highway departments. By writing to the department of transportation of the state in which you want to travel, or its office of tourism, you can usually receive a free map in advance. Service stations' road maps are now often sold at a low price. Chamber of Commerce offices and local tourism offices usually have official road maps free.

Highway maps include more information than most of us realize. The best part of the map to start with is the legend, which tells you what all the symbols mean. It also tells you something about the nature of the highways, because different classes of roads are marked with lines of different sizes, designs and colors. Four-lane interstate highways are easily distinguished from country roads. The more scenic roads are often overprinted with a wide yellow band.

Before me, as I write this, is the most recent official highway map for New Mexico, and the longer I study it, the more I want to go. All state and national park areas are marked. So are the extensive national forest areas. Indian reservations are easily located because they are printed in yellow. Mountain ranges are indicated and elevation of peaks and passes are printed in. All of this is important information for a bicyclist.

There is also a table of distances between cities, as well as a quick-reference mileage chart. Bicycle travelers can judge the relative sizes of towns and cities and avoid major centers of population.

The state doesn't let the back side of the maps go to waste. Here I find a list of New Mexico's historic churches, a complete list of state parks, campgrounds, and monuments, including their facilities and attractions, added information on visiting Indian reservations, ski areas (high country and steep grades expected) hunting and fishing details, and a complete list of museums found along the highways. Also, there is an inset map with special legends showing the historic trails of the state, a device that enables the touring cyclist traveling New Mexico to know when he is following the route of Coronado or pedaling along the Camino Real.

State highway maps, however, have their limitations. There are usually many roads not shown on them, especially little country roads, leading to quiet settlements and scenic rural areas where the rider can escape people pressure. In the West especially, many such roads are unpaved. One way to learn about the back roads is to stop at the county courthouse and ask for a county map, usually from the county engineer's office. This map may sell for fifty cents or a dollar. If you are going to spend some time exploring the area, the map will be worth many times the price. If you belong to an automobile club, you can receive its maps. The special route maps they provide, however, are designed for automobile travel.

The most detailed and accurate maps of all for showing physical features of the landscape are the topographic maps published by the U. S. Geological Survey. These have brown contour lines drawn in, usually at every twenty-foot elevation. Where the lines are close together, the slope is obviously a steep one. Once you study the legends, these maps will reveal such features as dwellings, trails, tunnels, marshes, railroads, ruins and lighthouses. The problem with topo maps is that the large scale, which permits them to show the landscape in such detail, means that each map covers a relatively small area and anyone on a bike tour of more than a few hours can find himself off the map. This means carrying too many maps on the long tour. But the topo maps can be used for planning at home in advance.

Some city libraries have map rooms where you may examine topo maps at your leisure. You can also order individual maps directly from the U. S. Geological Survey, or buy them over the counter at one of its outlet stores or at a government printing office bookstore. Checking the phone book may show that these maps are available in your city. In some cities they can be purchased at the city hall for local areas. The national distribution center for the eastern United States is USGS, 12201 Sunrise Valley Drive, Reston, VA 22092. This office will supply a free key to all the topo maps for the United States, enabling you to order the individual maps you need to buy. For areas west of the Mississippi River, write U. S. Geological Survey, Denver Federal Center, Denver, CO 80225.

You will save time if you not only study the map in advance, but also mark your route. A yellow marking pen will enable you to read the map features beneath the transparent ink. Then, with your map folded to fit into a clear pocket on top of your handlebar bag, you can check it at a glance.

COMPASS

You may not need a compass where population is heavy, towns are close together and signposts abound. But in thinly populated regions, you may not see a direction indicator for miles, and the sun may be hidden by clouds. On these occasions a glance at a compass can keep you on the route.

If you want a better-grade compass, suitable for canoeing, hiking, hunting or cross-country skiing as well, look for one that has an azimuth scale for obtaining readings with greater accuracy. It should also have a sighting device plus a way to adjust the compass to compensate for declination. Keep in mind that magnetic north will vary depending on the part of the country you are traveling through. If you are going to stick to well-marked highways, an inexpensive pocket compass will be sufficient.

RANCH COUNTRY HAZARDS

Some years ago ranchers and farmers found a way to avoid having to open and shut all those gates that keep livestock where they belong. Instead of gates, they began digging pits in the

City parks and quiet streets offer friends the opportunity to ride together for the pleasure of pedaling. SCHWINN BICYCLE COMPANY PHOTO.

roads and covering these with a grate made of rails, lengths of heavy steel pipe or planks turned on edge. Between the crossbars they left a space to discourage the cows from attempting to cross the grates. The idea works. Ranch and farm vehicles can cross easily enough, as cattle guards are at ground level and extend from one edge of the road to the other, forming a barrier about four feet wide. They are sometimes found on public roads, too, especially in the West.

Even though cattle guards are at ground level, you can still spot them well in advance by looking at the fences. If the road goes through a gap in the fence where there is no gate, chances are excellent that there is a cattle guard.

In this case, the only safe procedure is to stop and walk your bike over the cattle guard. Otherwise you could wreck or bend a wheel or even the frame.

CITY TOURING

City automobile traffic, with its trucks, buses and local heavy-footed jockeys, can turn a trip into a survival test. The bicyclist should do some advance thinking about the city routes he or she will follow, and the time of day they will be encountered. City maps, which service stations sometimes post on their walls, can be helpful since they point out major thruways, which are to be avoided. It is also wise to stay far enough from these main routes to avoid traffic feeding onto them from tributary streets. This can be especially important during the rush hours. These especially busy hours come from seven to nine in the morning and again late in the afternoon, between four and six. Noon traffic can also become sticky. Midmorning and midafternoons are the best times to negotiate the cities and avoid heavy traffic. The best time of all is on Sunday, especially in the morning.

Truck routes should also be avoided. Secondary state routes are sometimes good bets for the bicycling tourist, and a map will warn you if part of the route combines with truck routes or major thruways.

If you want to miss a city entirely, this can sometimes be managed by cutting off on state highways. Study the highway map carefully to be sure in advance that the route you've chosen goes all the way and that there are bridges where you need to cross rivers.

Bicyclists sharing the road with motor vehicles should ride single file and close to the right-hand side of the road. FLORIDA NEWS BUREAU PHOTO.

BIKE AND CAR COMBINATION

Increasingly, automobile tourists take along bicycles, strapped to racks on their vehicles. The bikes have a special role and can enrich your travel experiences. They are an excellent way to tour park or forest roads once you have arrived at your destination. Park the car, unshackle the bikes and see the countryside at your leisure. These tours within tours can be an hour's ride or an overnight trip that eventually brings you back to the family motor vehicle. This system works especially well in certain national parks.

You can also combine your bicycle touring with hiking. For trail hikes that bring you back to the bike by the end of the day you carry only a day pack for lunch, rain gear, a bird guide and whatever else you take along on such outings. Take care to lock your bikes to a tree or some other substantial anchor point, because today's vacation areas are hunting grounds for thieves. Not many years ago, campers left tents and equipment for a day of roaming, fully expecting to find their possessions untouched when they returned. No more. Take every precaution and remember that bicycles in transit should be locked on their carrying racks as well.

TRAVEL COMPANIONS

If you are going to travel with companions, choose the group carefully. A bicycle trip can turn otherwise compatible people into adversaries. Those touring together should have similar pedaling abilities so the pace set by one is comfortable to the other, hour after hour, or they should have no objection to pedaling alone and meeting at the day's end.

In addition, good traveling companions are blessed with a sense of humor, not necessarily fun and jokes, but the ability to accept bad weather, flat tires and headwinds without continual grumbling. Short trips together can tell you something about each other's riding habits and personalities before starting out on a long tour. In the planning stage, settle on destination and, if possible, the routes to follow. Then, if you should become separated, each member of the group can find his or her way alone. There should also be agreement about the kinds of accommodations you will seek out along the way. Will you camp all the way, or will you stay in a motel occasionally? What about meals, especially restaurant meals that will cut into the budget? Open and frank discussions of these points in advance will eliminate reasons for dissension along the trail.

Rest stops give bicycle tourists an opportunity to check tires, brakes and other parts to be certain that their bicycles are still in top condition. FLORIDA NEWS BUREAU PHOTO.

TOURING IS FOR FAMILIES

When Pete and Bonnie Kutschenreuter were still relative newcomers to the world of bicycling, they began dreaming of pedaling across the continent—from the West Coast to their home in Loveland, Ohio, on the edge of Cincinnati. From the beginning there were some strong arguments against this trip. They had two young children, ages three and five, who had to be carried, one on each of their bikes. "My parents," Bonnie told me, "would have kept the children, but we didn't want to leave them behind." Their bicycles, at that stage in their riding, were five-speeds which they traded in for ten-speeds for the trip through Rocky Mountain country. The Kutschenreuters, however, were determined to have this adventure, and because they felt strongly about taking their children, they began making careful and detailed plans.

From the beginning they realized that they could not carry both children and camping equipment on the bicycles. So they arranged with a neighborhood teenager, a good driver, to drive their equipment-loaded station wagon.

They then had to plan their route across the country. The Bikecentennial route had not yet been mapped. "I had never been to the Pacific Northwest," Bonnie says, "so we decided to start from Everett, Washington." This made the total trip back to Cincinnati 2,700 miles. Pete Kutschenreuter arranged to be away from work for two months and the family loaded everything into their station wagon and headed west to their jumping-off point.

Once they started the bicycle tour, "We carried

Families who bicycle together should plan rides that are fashioned to the abilities of the least experienced member. SCHWINN BICYCLE COMPANY PHOTO.

Parents can condition their children to bicycling early in life if they are willing to carry the extra weight. It is important to make sure that the child's seat is comfortable and safe. U. S. DEPARTMENT OF TRANSPORTATION PHOTO, JAMES CARROLL.

what we would need for the day," says Pete. "We had to have lunch as well as items the children would need." Their driver passed them once each day. They told him where they would be at the end of the day, and he had campsites arranged for them when they arrived. He also carried an aerosol can of green paint, with which he sprayed an occasional guiding arrow on the road.

In this manner the Kutschenreuters pedaled through Washington, on into the Rockies and back East toward home, covering about fifty miles a day and seeing America as they never had before. They made hundreds of color pictures, which they later used in giving talks to bicycle clubs and other groups. The Kutschenreuters look back on their trip as an exciting adventure which they would not have missed. They later graduated to lighter-weight ten-speed bicycles and continued to use their bicycles for touring, commuting and errands around home. Pete became president of the League of American Wheelmen and their children, understandably, became serious riders early in life. Pete and Bonnie still give talks about their big trip across the country while thinking about other trips they expect to make.

Family touring means adapting equipment lists to meet the needs of children as they grow. Those who take babies on tours have to survey the choice of backpack carriers, trailers and toddler seats. They talk with others who have used the equipment and finally make their own personal selections. The first consideration is always the safety of the child. The parent must consider whether he or she is skilled enough in bicycling to ride safely with the added weight, or whether more experience and training is needed before the family undertakes any tour, even a one-day venture.

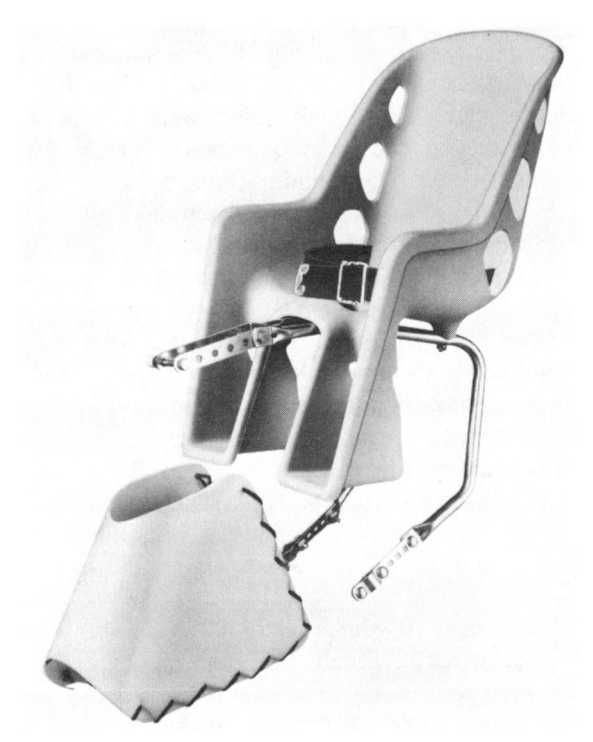

Child carrier with a steel frame and a leg and foot protector. TROXEL MANUFACTURING COMPANY PHOTO.

CHILD TRANSPORT

Adding an infant seat to any bicycle introduces new demands on the cyclist. The bike will not handle as easily. The common choice is a seat that fits behind the pedaler so that the child rides facing forward. This position puts less wind on the child. The baby should be strapped in. There is a genuine danger of small feet getting caught in the spokes of the rear wheel, but there are lightweight, low-cost plastic aprons that fit the back of the bike and keep feet out of the wheels.

Other baby seats fit on the front of the bike. One kind fits in front of the handlebars. If the baby faces forward in this position, it has a maximum view. If it faces backward, it has a good position for keeping contact and carrying on conversation with the parent. But the front seat puts the baby into a hazardous situation in case of a head-on collision and also makes heavier work of steering. The smaller the baby, the greater the need for high sides on the seat and for a high back to support and protect the head and neck.

TRAILERS

One elderly rider we met in Texas had pedaled his two-wheeler from Maine and was planning to go on to Mexico, then start back. His was a leisurely trip. He had already been gone from home for six months and was not exactly certain what the total length of his trip might be. He felt that he needed more equipment than he could carry comfortably by draping bags from his bicycle, front and rear, so he was using a trailer. He insisted that he was getting along fine with the extra wheels.

Trailers that are suitably light in weight are available. But they turn the bicycle into a different breed of machine altogether, especially on the downgrades. Braking on the downhill slopes is touchy with a trailer. One reason is the added weight. Another is that even in a slight turn, the trailer tends to make the rear wheel slide sideways. Again, whether to include a bike trailer in your touring plans is a personal decision, but not one that should be made lightly if there is any hope at all of trimming the load to fit on two wheels.

Trailers are gaining popularity for transporting one or two small children behind either a standard bicycle or a tandem.

ON THE FREEWAYS

Stretched across America is the world's finest highway system, a spiderweb of pavements connecting anyone with everywhere. The crowning achievement of the highway builders is a system of freeways which provides multi-lane highways with wide median strips separating traffic. This system began in 1944 with passage of the Federal Highway Act. As a result, we can drive coast to coast with scarcely a traffic light to slow us down. Those freeways are flanked by wide, smooth shoulders that get almost no use unless a disabled vehicle must pull out of traffic. Seeing these shoulders, we wonder if they could not also be used by touring bicyclists.

Increasingly, bicyclists are asking why the freeways are closed to non-motorized traffic. California now has hundreds of miles of freeway shoulders where bicycles are allowed. In addition, the state plans to open additional miles of freeways to its bicyclists.

It is up to bicyclists to start such action. Highway engineers typically want to vote the idea down. But there is a growing conviction that bicyclists have the same rights that motorists have —a right to reach all points served by public highways. Barring them from a highway limits that right and sometimes creates a hardship.

Are superhighways more hazardous for cyclists than other roads? This, according to John Finley Scott, President of the California Association of Bicycling Organizations, "is simply not borne out by current safety data." He says, "Additionally, there are good reasons to believe that freeway travel is, in many cases, safer for the cyclists than travel on parallel non-freeway routes."

One of the fears among some cyclists is that vehicles, overtaking them from the rear, might overrun them. Recent safety studies show that accidents of that type are uncommon unless either the bicycle or the motor vehicle is turning or crossing the other's path. On freeways there is relatively little of this maneuvering. One trouble

The open roads near Boulder, Colorado, are highly popular with touring cyclists. Note how this rider has equipped her bike for a full day's ride. COURTESY HARTLEY ALLEY, THE TOURING CYCLIST SHOP.

spot could be around the ramps. Some ramps have light traffic much of the time and cyclists need to understand the hazards involved in crossing high-volume on-and-off ramps, dismount when necessary, and wait for a break in oncoming traffic.

Also there is the fear that, once bicycles are permitted, children will begin making use of the freeways for playing on their bicycles. There are efforts in some areas to find ways of limiting freeway bicycle traffic to mature riders.

One leader of the California Association of Bicycling Organizations says, "We recommend that all California freeways should be open to cyclists except where the freeway is clearly more dangerous than a feasible alternate route. Where there is no alternate route, the freeway should be open regardless of the hazard." The right to travel, by whatever means, say these West Coast bicyclists, is fundamental. Other states are likely to face this problem as traveling bicyclists increase in numbers in the years ahead.

WET WEATHER TIPS

At times, traveling bicyclists get caught out in the rain or snow. In some areas, including parts of the Pacific Northwest, and in some seasons, there is likely to be rain almost any time. The answer is to prepare yourself. Fast riding on wet surfaces is hazardous. Personally, I deal with rain by getting out of it when possible. You can keep a surprising amount of water off yourself by taking shelter under a tree with dense foliage. Remember *not* to take shelter beneath one isolated tree if you are caught in an electrical storm. In this case, wet is wise because of the threat of lightning. I have often seen a rider stop, lean his or her bike against a tree, whip a lightweight plastic sheet from a pannier and use it to cover both rider and bike, so that both stay dry until ready to roll again. Once the plastic is shaken to eliminate excess water, it is tucked into a plastic bag so that it doesn't get other equipment wet.

The condition of tires and brakes is especially important in determining how safely and efficiently you ride on wet roads. The smoother the tire, the less traction on wet surfaces. The usual rib pattern found on most tires gives a good grip on wet pavement, but if you ride in the rain frequently you may want to switch to a pattern with tread extending down farther on the sidewalls. Either the bee's nest or herringbone pattern gives good traction.

The brake systems least affected by rain are coaster brakes, because they are enclosed in the hubs, and disk brakes, which also have protected working parts. This, however, does not cover the majority of us, who ride bicycles equipped with caliper brakes. These models stop the machine by pressing brake pads against the wheel rims, and the brake pads work best against clean, dry rims.

Your riding techniques can be more important than the kind of bicycle you pedal. Many of the techniques essential to safe riding in wet weather are similar to those involved in driving a car under the same conditions. Remember that you will need more distance for stopping on wet streets. How much more depends on speed, weight, ability of tires to gain traction, condition of brakes, and how you use your brakes. You may find that the brakes need considerably greater pressure to bring you to a stop when the surface is wet. It is important to look ahead and anticipate hazards. Wet-weather riding is not the most relaxing brand of travel on a bicycle. The rider must concentrate all the time.

In addition, it is important to develop a sensitivity, a feel, for the movements of your bicycle so you can anticipate slides before they occur and take early steps to correct them. When the surface is wet, your bicycle is likely to slide on the curves. The road can be especially slippery during the early part of a rainstorm following a long dry spell. Oil and dirt collect on the streets, and nothing short of a half hour of hard rain may wash the pavement clean. Autumn, when leaves begin to drift down onto the streets, brings a special hazard, because wet leaves can cause you to skid. It's best to take it easy if the pavement is wet. Then, if you should begin to slide, remember to correct the slide by turning into it instead of jerking the handlebars away from the direction of the slide.

In general, riding on wet streets, like driving automobiles on wet streets, calls for making no sudden changes in direction or speed. Sudden changes can cause a slide that brings on a spill. Braking may not be the best response to skidding. Maintaining an even pressure on the pedals may correct the situation and help keep you moving along on a straight course.

DESERT RIDING

This country's splendid deserts are among its treasured landscapes, and bicycling through them can be unforgettable. But riding through desert landscapes has its dangers, and if your tour leads into the deserts you should give advance thought to potential problems.

The Great American Desert extends over large sections of the Southwestern states and south into Mexico. It is made up of four noted subdivisions, each a desert in itself. The Great Basin Desert lies between the Rocky Mountains and the Sierra Nevadas from central Oregon to Wyoming and southward into Utah and Nevada. Grasslands and sagebrush stretch across it, proving that not all desert is lifeless, blowing sand, as we have sometimes been conditioned to believe. (By definition, desert is land that receives ten inches or less of water per year.) The Chihuahuan Desert covers parts of Texas, New Mexico and Mexico—hot, dry cactus country. Then there is the Sonoran Desert, stretching over parts of southern California, Arizona and Mexico. Among the marks of this desert is the biggest cactus in the world, the saguaro, which sometimes reaches 50 feet in height, weighs 10 tons and lives more than 250 years. The Mohave, primarily in California and Nevada, is best known for Death Valley, where the National Park Service maintains one of the most remarkable of all vacation spots. Part of Death Valley lies 282 feet below sea level and the temperature there once rose on a summer day to 134° F. Death Valley is perhaps the hottest place on earth.

Riding through such country can only be done comfortably and safely by those willing to face a few facts of desert life. Your schedule in desert country should let you take advantage of the most comfortable traveling hours, early in the day. At night the desert air cools, often dramatically. The bicyclist takes advantage of this by getting on the road as soon as there is enough light to make travel safe. The best plan is to lay over in the shade during the heat of the day. Plan to reach a settlement or at least a source of water before midday. Spring is a favorite season for desert travel. The hot days of summer have not yet settled on the land. And if winter rains have been plentiful, there is likely to be a spring flower display of brilliant reds, yellows and purples. Even Death Valley, in some years, has fields of wild flowers, and travelers can check with park rangers to determine the spring flower timing before starting for the desert.

How you dress is doubly important in riding through desert country. Contrary to what you may think, this is not the place to begin shedding clothes and absorbing sunshine. Take along a long-sleeve shirt, preferably of lightweight, light-colored cotton, to protect yourself. Also equip yourself with a hat that has a brim wide enough to shade your face and neck. Again white is preferred because it reflects heat. Hikers and bicyclists often dip their hats, and sometimes their shirts as well, in water whenever they have the opportunity and wear them wet to help keep the body cool. In the dry air of the desert, however, this is a short-term luxury. You may also need lightweight pants, instead of shorts, especially if you sunburn easily.

Since the body loses water rapidly when you are riding through hot, dry desert country, you must carry enough water to replace that loss. At least two water bottles should be included in your equipment; another and perhaps larger bottle can be fastened to the carrier. Regardless of the amount of water carried, the rider has to plan his trip carefully, from one watering stop to the next. In addition, consumption of water must be paced to make the supply last. You never know when a tire repair job or other emergency might keep you out longer than you planned.

A supply of salt tablets is a good idea if your doctor agrees, and be alert for early signs of heat stroke or heat exhaustion in yourself or another member of your group. The hotter the day, the slower your cadence should be and the more frequent your rest periods. Overexertion can help bring on physical troubles.

Winds can be strong in desert country, especially during the afternoon. On occasion, you may run into sandstorms, which not only make riders uncomfortable, but can cause severe damage to the working parts of bicycles.

There are lessons to be learned from the animals that live in the desert. Wild creatures survive in deserts, not because they shape the deserts to their needs or ignore its limiting conditions, but because they themselves adapt. During the hottest hours, the jackrabbit rests in the shade of a cactus, the kangaroo rat sleeps in the coolness of its underground shelter, and the reptiles simply wait in the shade for cooler evening hours. The more severe the conditions, the more vital it becomes for wild creatures to make concessions, and this is a rule that bicyclists might keep in mind.

MOUNTAIN RIDING

Climbing mountains on a bicycle is a challenge both physically and psychologically. At the outset, the climb may seem overwhelming, the mountain stretching on forever into the clouds. But this is exactly the way *not* to think about it. The mountains *can* be pedaled, and experienced riders seek them out as trophies. The highest paved highway in the country goes up Mt. Evans in Colorado to 14,264 feet, and bicyclists do ride it to the top.

Before you start riding through the rugged mountain country, however, whether it be the Appalachians, the Rockies or the Sierra Nevadas, you should accept the fact that pedaling up mountains is going to be slow and demanding. There is no penalty for getting off your bicycle on occasion. Walking the bicycle is not, or at least should not be, a disgrace. If you need to rest, stop and do so, remembering that a brief rest is better than a prolonged stop. The secret is to set a sensible pace for yourself. Start up at a speed that is neither sluggish nor too fast, then maintain your pace. Do not worry about how you compare with other riders. Set your own pace. Then use your gears to make the machine do maximum work as the climb becomes more difficult.

THE DOWNHILL

Touring through mountain country reconfirms what we always knew: mountains have two sides, and the hill you pedal up leads to a downhill run on the other side. That downhill run can be the memorable part of the day. The temptation is to turn the bike loose. The wind is in your face and your wheels spin as never before. Besides, you know you earned this ride the hard way.

Approach that downhill run with a touch of caution. First, take a little time out to rest on the top. Get your breath and cool off. This puts both mind and body into condition for the coming run. If you are sweating from the uphill ride, the rest at the top is especially important.

This is also the time to check your bicycle again. You may have noticed some little irregularity on the uphill climb. Investigate it and make repairs or adjustments if needed. Check the brakes, handlebars and tires, and see that bags are secure. Then, when the rider and the bicycle are both in readiness, turn the bicycle downhill. It is a good idea to keep sunglasses on so the wind won't make you half blind from watering eyes.

Blowouts while going down steep hills are a possibility. If the back tire goes flat, you can probably handle the machine and bring it to a safe halt. This is not so easy with a flat front tire. With a flat on the front, try to stop using only the rear brake. Also try not to swerve or turn with a flat front tire. The tire loses its grip when it loses air, and turning will throw the rider.

Descending a steep hill is one time when it may be wise to lay aside the old rule about hugging the side of the road so you are out of the way of other vehicles. The possibilities of an accident increase if you are running on the edge of the road and have to swerve to miss gravel or trash. You may be thrown onto the shoulder where, even if you stay upright, you can damage a tire. The best thing to do, depending on traffic, is to stay in the middle of the lane on descents, giving yourself room to maneuver in either direction if the need arises. Watch out for automobiles rounding sharp curves and overtaking you from the rear.

Most mountainous roads have curves, and they are not banked to keep bicycles on the road at high speed. Keep your hands on the brakes. It is a good idea to apply the brakes from time to time to be certain that everything is under control. You may pick up speed faster than you realize, especially if your bicycle is heavily loaded, and wind up rolling along at 50 miles an hour or faster. Exciting and exhilarating, yes—but high speeds can be extremely hazardous, especially if you come upon a rough or dirty stretch of highway, or round a curve and encounter a situation you didn't expect. Nobody wants to take a downhill tumble at high speed. This is why experienced riders keep their bikes under full control all the way—even though they whip along at speeds that make the downhill ride one to talk about later in camp.

BEARS AND BIKERS

There are still a few wild places in this country where the person traveling and sleeping outdoors must be concerned about wild animals—even bears. Most of today's problem bears are found in national parks, especially Yellowstone, Yosemite, Glacier and the Great Smokies. In recent years the National Park Service, increasingly nervous about the accident potential of people-bear encounters, has taken steps to move the bears back away from the roads. Not many years ago, tourists traveling through these parks could expect to see bears. They were especially numerous around campgrounds and picnic areas. Today, the Park Service uses "bear-proof" garbage cans to frustrate hungry bears, and the individual bear that becomes a chronic nuisance will be moved.

Despite precautions, campers staying in bear country may find themselves sharing an occasional campsite with a black bear. Even a grizzly is a possibility in Yellowstone or Glacier. Where there is any chance at all of bears coming to your campground, there are precautionary steps you must take.

First, remember that food attracts bears. They are omnivorous, just as bicycle riders are. Besides, they have a sense of smell far superior to ours. They can sense the presence of food for hundreds of yards. Never keep food in your tent or near where you sleep. One bicyclist, touring the Blue Ridge Parkway, awakened to find his bicycle gone. It was located nearby, badly damaged. A bear had dragged it off to get the food left in the attached panniers.

Put food into a plastic sack that will seal in odors, then hang it from a tree limb well above the bear's reach, away from tent or sleeping bag. With bears, as with any other wildlife, the best course is to keep a respectful distance at all times and remember that you are an invader in the wild animal's living area.

Bears are not the only creatures that might threaten people who camp in wild places. Any wild animal that has grown too accustomed to people and lost its fear of them can attack and cause injury. This includes moose, deer, bison and elk, often seen in national or state parks. It also includes skunks as well as any animal, large or small, that seems too trusting or tame. Tidbits from your food pack corrupt wildlife. Getting along with wildlife, whether bears or butterflies, is a matter of attitude and of learning to fit quietly into the wild world, becoming a part of the scene rather than an intruder.

GORP, ANYONE?

People who travel under their own energy need frequent refueling as surely as motor-driven machines do. This is why hikers and touring bicyclists often have a bag of gorp within reach. The recipe for this high-energy supplement depends upon the maker's taste and on what is available. Here is a basic gorp plan that will do nicely if you have no special recipe of your own.

Start by mixing together equal parts of peanuts, raisins and nonmelting chocolate bits (M&Ms are the usual choice). To this you may add, as you choose, granola, coconut, miniature marshmallows, cereals and dried fruits.

FUN AND GAMES

Remember that there will be times when you have nothing to do but rest and relax, and even though you are traveling light, you may want to include a few items to enliven these periods. A deck of cards takes little space, and a Frisbee weighs only ounces. Or you may want to pack a sketch pad and pencils, or even watercolors. A magnifying glass is handy along the nature trails. A book of crossword puzzles is worth considering, and so is a small songbook. Paperback books travel well on bicycles, and you can trade within your group or at used-book shops.

TIPS FOR TOUR LEADERS

Every organized trip should have one experienced bicyclist in charge. Although the tour need not be organized down to the last detail, there will be occasions calling for a leader's decision. The following suggestions for trip planning and leading come from riders of long experience.

If your group consists of more than a few riders, travel the route in advance of the ride. The closer you can make this to the actual day of the ride, the better, because there is less possibility of being surprised by detours, bridge closings or roads turned too rough for comfort and safety. The best way to inspect the route is by bicycle; the second best is by car.

Prepare a single-sheet handout giving information on the route. Include a map if possible. Information should include the length of the trip in miles and hours, as well as the time of departure and the estimated time of return and plans for lunch.

While choosing the route, also select rest stops. Good places for rest stops include the top of a difficult hill, major changes in route direction and places offering shade, pleasant scenery and convenient parking areas for bicycles, off the highway. Remember that more stops may be needed in hot weather or when your group includes riders who are not in top condition.

The leader should also carry a tire pump, a repair kit and a chain-repair kit. There should also be at least one first-aid kit.

As riders assemble for the trip, introduce those who might not know each other. You may also want to look over the bicycles brought for the trip. Pick one experienced rider to bring up the rear so you will know that everyone is with you. It is possible to lose riders once the bicycles are strung out along the highway: if there are road junctions where directions might be confusing, explain these to the riders before setting off and suggest marking them on the maps. In case of rain, the leader decides whether or not the trip is "go." Members of the group should stay close enough together to prevent riders from making wrong turns.

Where traffic is fairly heavy, travel single file; never ride more than two abreast. The lead bicyclist should be able to maintain a steady pace. The leader may want to stop and let the group pass to see that there are no serious problems. Rest stops should allow the slower riders time, not only to catch up with the leaders, but also to rest. Otherwise, those most in need of rest may make the whole tour without meaningful rest stops, and this can sour riders on group trips quickly.

If there is a breakdown, the group should either stop until repairs are completed, or another rider or two should stay behind to help.

13. THE CAMPING CYCLIST

The least costly way to live while on a bicycle tour is to camp. This kind of living is a test of your self-sufficiency, but it's fun once you get used to living outdoors.

Successful bike camping begins with selecting equipment you will carry. If you are going to travel the easy way, i.e., accompanied by a sag wagon, weight and bulk are not serious problems. The sag wagon can transport a heavy family-style tent that may have been purchased originally for auto camping trips. There is also room in the accompanying vehicle for more comforts and a complete camp kitchen.

Most bicycle campers, however, expect to be self-sufficient, living with only what they can pack on their bicycles. Ounces count. The challenge is to cut weight to a minimum, leaving behind all items not really needed, but carrying along enough to be comfortable on the road. Some things are essential, and the safest plan is to make an initial checklist, then begin assembling equipment.

Your checklist can be organized into shelter, bedding, food, cooking equipment, tools, clothing, personal items and incidentals. The checklist can vary from one traveler to the next, and probably will, but here is a list that will do as a start, and that can be adapted to your own needs. If it seems to have more items than you would use, remember that this is a list of reminders designed to keep you from overlooking essentials; you can adjust this master list to your own idea of what is essential.

CHECKLIST FOR BICYCLE TOURING

Shelter
tent, tube, tarp
ground cloth
tent stakes
tent repair kit
ropes

Bedding
sleeping bag
pad or air mattress
waterproof sack for bag

Cooking Equipment
stove
fuel container
spare stove parts
skillet
stew pot with handle
coffee pot
aluminum foil
tongs
knife
fork
spoon
cup

Tools and Parts
bicycle repair kit
tire pump
tire repair kit
chain rivet remover
roll tape
crescent wrench
spoke tool
spokes
spare tire
chain link

Clothing

men
trousers
shirt
sweater
windbreaker
rain gear
hat
dress shoes
riding shoes
bathing suit
four sets underwear
shirts for riding
shorts
riding socks
dress socks

women
blouses
riding shorts
riding socks
riding shoes
dress shoes
pantyhose
1 pair slacks
skirts
underwear
rain outfit
hat
bathing suit
pajamas
windbreaker
sweater

Personal
towel
washcloth
soap
toothbrush
toothpaste
first aid kit
razor
sunglasses
suntan lotion
chapstick
styptic pencil
after shave
comb

FIRST THE BACKYARD

If you are new to bicycle camping, or if your equipment is untested, check your gear out before leaving on your trip. You can do this in the backyard. The test run will give you the opportunity to discover in advance any little surprises that you otherwise might encounter for the first time as darkness comes on at the end of a long day of pedaling.

The tent, especially, should be checked out in advance. Set it up and see that all the parts are there and that you know how to assemble them. When erected, the tent should be neat and tight, with no loose fabric that billows in the wind.

In addition, check out the stove you will carry and see that it works satisfactorily and that you understand it.

TENTS

Wonderful things have happened in the world of lightweight tenting. Until recent times the typical tent was heavy canvas, usually either a drab gray or green, and weighing more than anyone wants to carry on a bicycle. It was often difficult for anyone but the manufacturer's public relations person to set up, and it was designed more for week-long outings than for the one-night stops of backpackers and bicyclists. In the camping world of today you see roomy little tents that weigh only a few pounds and can be erected quickly and painlessly. Furthermore, these modern tents come in pleasing colors and ingenious designs. What this means for the bicyclists is that recent trends in camping equipment have made longer bicycle trips possible with comfort assured.

The best place to begin looking at the variety of tents is in a wilderness supply store or backpacker's outfitting shop. If you are also a backpacker, you probably already have the tent you will need for bicycle camping. Tent merchandisers learned years ago that the best of all ways to display these shelters is to set them up on the showroom floor. You should, if possible, see the tent set up before you buy it, and if the salesman is willing to demonstrate the process of erecting the tent, or taking it down, you can get a good idea of how easy it is to handle, pack in its sack and carry on a bicycle.

You will also be able to judge whether or not the size of the tent fits your needs. Many of the lightweight tents on the market are designed to accommodate two people in sleeping bags. These tents are also suitable for individual use; they are lightweight enough to be transported by one person, and the added space gives room to keep one's pack and panniers under cover and out of the weather.

Inspect the general design of the tent. Some models are roomier than others and permit you to sit up with comfort. This is especially true of the dome designs. The added headroom enables campers to change clothes with greater ease than in the little A-frames or pup tents. Space is also important if bad weather confines you to the tent or keeps you inside during meals.

Tent designers now recognize that ventilation is important. Small windows near the top give warm air an escape route, and windows in two or more sides of the tent help provide for cross-ventilation. Some tents have large windows and you may want to consider these, especially if you will be touring in warmer regions. Windows should be screened and protected with zippered flaps that can be opened or closed from the inside as the need arises.

Your tent should keep water off you not only from above, but also from beneath the tent. Campers no longer dig drainage ditches around their tents—or at least they shouldn't. Ditching is contrary to the rules in most campgrounds, and with good reason. It scars the landscape and gives erosion a starting place. Instead rely on a tent with a waterproof floor. This flooring should extend up the walls of the tent all around, for six or eight inches.

You will also be interested in learning how the tent is supported. It should come complete with its own poles or supporting frame. Some modern tents have lightweight frames built into sleeves that are part of them. Others have external frames that can be fastened together to form a support beneath which the tent is attached. Some have internal poles or frames. The tents that need no guy ropes or tent stakes to keep them erect are especially appealing to bicycle campers. If you have to carry tent stakes, choose light-

Lightweight, two-person Gore-Tex touring tent. Sets up in one minute. Weighs 3¾ pounds. EARLY WINTERS, LTD.

weight aluminum or plastic ones. These can usually be pushed into the ground by hand. In windy country you may have to tie down a tent that does not ordinarily require guy ropes, or at least you may have to weight it down with your equipment bags.

Cotton cloth, the standard tenting material for hundreds of years, has gone out of favor for modern lightweight tents. Instead synthetics, especially nylon, have become the dominant tent materials. Nylon is lighter than treated cotton and is also mildew-proof. It does not rot, as cotton does, and it can even be stored and carried damp for limited times. No tent, however, should be stored wet for long. Even those made of synthetics may have cotton stitching that can be weakened by rot. It is a good plan to open your tent and shake it clean when returning from a trip, then leave it set up until it is thoroughly dry.

Tent fabric should, as campers say, "breathe." The human body gives off surprising amounts of moisture, and unless this moisture can escape through the fabric, it condenses on the inside of the tent and keeps tent and camper damp. Ideally, the fabric shuts out the rain while allowing water vapor to escape. This is difficult to accomplish with synthetics, so tentmakers commonly market tents complete with a covering fly to stretch over the tent. This double protection is especially helpful in weather when windows cannot be opened for ventilation, or in cold weather. Bicycle campers often prefer to take their chances with the weather and shave the weight on their packs by leaving the tent fly behind.

Tentmakers have been working toward development of a fabric that will both breathe and shut out the rain, so the fly can be eliminated. One available fabric designed to accomplish this is Gore-Tex. This is a super-thin film of synthetic material which can be adapted for outdoor use by bonding it to nylon. Although Gore-Tex may still permit some condensation on the inside of tents and the material is not yet flame resistant, it is a big step in the right direction.

You should inspect the stitching used in sewing the tent parts together. The quality of the stitching can provide a clue to overall tent quality. The seams should be double-stitched with lock stitching. For maximum strength, fabric edges should be folded over and the edges lapped into a locking position, then stitched. Zippers should be heavy-duty.

It is possible (you learn this during your first rainstorm) that the tent seams have not been treated with a sealing material. Manufacturers often leave this for the customer. Before you use it, treat the seams of your new tent with a sealer purchased in a tube from an outdoor-supply or sporting goods store. Allow the sealer to dry for several hours. Read the directions carefully before using this material, in part because it can be hazardous. While you are treating the tent seams, you may also want to seal the seams on your bike packs, as well as your nylon parka or jacket.

Some bike campers travel without tents and take their chances with the weather. You win some and you lose some. My suggestion is not to go on a camping trip without some kind of shelter to stretch over your sleeping bag. A dark, wet night can be very long. There are, however, substitutes you may want to consider for a tent. One is the tent tube. This is a plastic tube big enough to provide room for a sleeping bag. It is set up by stretching a line through it, then tying the rope between two trees. The ends of the tube are usually open for ventilation, so the tube admits a certain amount of rain as well as insects in search of bitable people. At best, the tent tube is less than comfortable and not very good protection.

At the least, a camper should go equipped with a lightweight fly or tarp that can be rigged to cover the sleeping bag and packs, and perhaps even your bicycle. A sheet of plastic will work for this purpose, providing it is thick enough to stand up under whipping by the wind and repeated folding and packing.

If you want to cut the cost of your camping equipment, consider assembling your own tent. The following companies specialize in kits.

Altra Inc., 5441 Western Avenue, Boulder, CO 80301

Frostline Kits, Frostline Circle, Denver, CO 80241

Holubar Mountaineering, Ltd., Box 7, Boulder, CO 80306

The following companies sell ready-to-use lightweight tents through their mail order departments.

Eastern Mountain Sports, Inc., Vose Farm Road, Peterborough, NH 03458

Eddie Bauer, 15010 NE 36th St., Redmond, WA 98052

L. L. Bean, Inc., Freeport, ME 04052

Bike Warehouse, 215 Main St., B4, New Middleton, OH 44442

Bishop-Freeman Co., 1600 Foster St., Evanston, IL 60204

Don Gleason's Camper's Supply, Inc., 59 Pearl St., P.O. Box 87, Northampton, MA 01060

Laacke & Joys, 1430 N. Water, Milwaukee, WI 53202

Moor and Mountain, 63 Park St., Andover, MA 01810

Recreational Equipment, Inc., P.O. Box C-88125, Seattle, WA 98140

Norm Thompson, 1805 NW Thurman, Portland, OR 97209

The Ski Hut, 1615 University, Berkeley, CA 94704

BIVOUAC COVER

Instead of packing along a tent, some riders carry a bivouac cover, which is simply a bag into which your sleeping bag fits. A good one will come with a bottom coated with waterproof materials, and will enhance the heating effectiveness of your sleeping bag by about 10 per cent. The top is generally made of breathable non-waterproof nylon or of Gore-Tex. For this reason, the bivouac cover is sometimes turned upside down as a substitute for a tent.

These bags come with grommets at the corners so they can be tied down. The weight is about a pound and a half and if you are not going to carry a tent, the bivouac cover definitely deserves consideration.

MATTRESS

Although some campers carry no mattress and insist that they can sleep through the night in comfort, even on a picnic table, most of us need a layer of softer material under the sleeping bag. There are two ways to go. You can select either an air mattress or a foam sleeping pad. In addition to providing a softer bed, the mattress or pad will give added insulation beneath a sleeping bag. (The bottom of the sleeping bag normally offers less insulation than the top, because the filler material is compressed by your body weight.) The foam pad should add only a pound or so to your load. The price of the foam pad is considerably lower than what you might pay for a good air mattress. It is, however, bulky to pack.

With an air mattress, you face the chore of inflating and deflating it. The easy way to inflate one of these mattresses by mouth is to spread it out on the ground or in your tent, then stretch out in a comfortable position beside it and begin breathing into it, instead of blowing. This way you rest while inflating your mattress.

With an air mattress there is always the possibility that it will deflate and let you down during the night. Properly handled, however, a good air mattress should last several seasons. Those made of nylon-coated fabric resist punctures best. Good air mattresses have tubular air cells, half a dozen of them, each running the length of the mattress and each equipped with its own valve. One punctured cell does not ruin a night's sleep.

SLEEPING BAGS

We've come a long way in outdoor equipment since wilderness trappers, using oversize safety pins, fastened their wool blankets together on cold nights to create the first sleeping bags. The sleeping bag has now become an absolute essential for outdoor living.

A sleeping bag does not provide warmth; instead, it conserves it by preventing loss of the heat generated by the human body. In other words, it insulates. How well it does this job depends first of all on the kind and quantity of material used as filler. The insulation comes from dead air trapped in the filler. If this material can be kept fluffy, it gives better insulation than when compressed.

The insulating materials you will be considering in choosing a sleeping bag are either down—the most efficient material—or synthetics. No one has yet invented a synthetic material that excels waterfowl down as an insulator. Down is the light, fluffy layer of feathers beneath the outer layer of the waterfowl's feathers. It evolved over millions of years and insulates waterfowl against the most severe cold weather.

The finest down comes from geese, but the amounts available are limited and for this reason the down, even in high-quality sleeping bags and garments, may be a combination of duck and goose down. There may also be a proportion of feathers in the mixture, but the more feathers included, the lower the insulating quality of the mix.

Down is odorless and nontoxic as well as being the lightest insulating material known. In addition it is breathable; water vapor coming off the body passes through the down. Otherwise, it would lose its insulating ability through compression. For this reason, the nylon covering on a good sleeping bag, whether it is filled with down or synthetics, is never waterproof.

One of the beauties of a down sleeping bag is that it can be compressed into a smaller space than the equivalent amount of insulation in the form of any other material. When the time comes to travel, you can force the sleeping bag into a remarkably small stuff sack. Then, when you set up camp at the end of the day, the sleeping bag fluffs right out again to its original bulk. This means that all those dead air spaces are working again to prevent heat loss. The best way to carry a down bag is not to roll it, but to push it into a stuff bag. In the bag, it assumes a different shape every time.

When checking down bags in the stores, give attention to the stitching pattern. A sleeping bag made by simply placing an uninterrupted layer of insulating material into a fabric envelope would soon prove worthless; the filler material would bunch up instead of staying spread out, providing even insulation. For this reason the insulation is held in place by one of a number of designs in stitching. The pattern used can be important in how well the bag insulates the sleeper against the cold.

The least expensive bags frequently have inner and outer coverings stitched together in tubes. Down is then blown into these spaces. But there is little or no insulation where the stitches come together. These bags may be all the protection needed for warm-weather camping. Other designs, including the slant beam pattern, provide better insulation.

Synthetic materials are less expensive than down, as you will realize when you begin shopping around. They are also bulkier in proportion to their ability to insulate. A good synthetic-filled sleeping bag may still meet your needs, though, especially for warm-weather touring. A sleeping bag carrying synthetic filler is going to weigh about a pound more than a down bag of comparable insulating qualities.

Synthetics, which have been improved greatly in recent years, do have one advantage over down: while down loses most of its insulating qualities when wet, the wet synthetics retain most of their ability to insulate. If you must sleep in a wet sleeping bag, you will do better if it is filled with a synthetic fiber.

The zipper on a sleeping bag, whether metal or plastic, provides an area where cold air can enter. To prevent this, quality sleeping bags have a sewn-in baffle—a strip of insulated material that covers the inside of the zipper and blocks the air.

Sleeping bags can be dry-cleaned or washed, following special directions. Most manufacturers recommend that down bags be washed in a front-opening machine, the kind without an agitator, found in laundromats. Use a light soap and no bleach and wash the bag on a gentle cycle. It should be rinsed several times to be certain that the soap is completely removed. The down tends to mat together during washing, but it can be put back into shape by tumble drying with a clean tennis shoe (which helps fluff the down) in a dryer set on low heat. If you decide to have the bag dry-cleaned, find a cleaner who has experience in handling these delicate jobs, because the wrong fluids can damage the bag.

The sleeping bag that gives the best protection for the weight is the mummy-shaped bag, but some campers find that the rectangular shapes provide so much more comfort that they are willing to carry the added weight and bulk. The mummy bag generally keeps the camper warmer because body heat is confined to a smaller space in it.

THE CAMP COOK

Touring cyclists learn to get along on plain foods, supplemented by nutritious snacks for keeping the energy level up. But for a long trip the camping bicyclist needs to provide for cooking hot meals, not only for better nutrition but also to help make the trip pleasant. This requires taking along a compact backpacker's stove. There are European models available in weights between one and two pounds. I have used both the Svea 123, a general favorite among backpackers, and the smaller model of the Optimus; both are satisfactory and both burn with an intensely hot flame. These little one-burners are capable of cooking complete, carefully planned meals.

Keep down the weight of kitchen equipment by making each pan do multiple chores. Use aluminum pans. Eating utensils can be tough plastic items that add minimum weight. Your pocket knife can replace a table knife at mealtime. An aluminum plate is satisfactory and a cup with detachable handle, both available in wilderness outfitting stores, will complete the basic equipment. You will need a plastic water bottle also, and you may want to add a few additional items to round out your own outfit. Until you have used your equipment a number of times you will not have a clear picture of exactly what best fits your needs, and because of this you may want to adjust the contents of your pack as you travel. Browse through the offerings of the stores that sell backpacking equipment and choose sparingly. This is no time to exercise your love of gadgets. What you are after is a camping outfit that does all the jobs that need doing, with a minimum of weight and bulk—a bare minimum.

PICKING A CAMPSITE

The best time to arrive at a campground is well ahead of darkness. This is advice that camping writers regularly offer to those who travel in motor vehicles, but it is especially important to bicycle tourists. A couple of hours of remaining daylight will give you time to select a good campsite. The earlier you arrive, the better the choice is going to be. If you roll into a campground late, there is always the possibility that the place will be filled already with campers.

If this happens, however, the bicyclist has an advantage that other campers usually can't expect. He needs little space, just enough to set up a small tent and park a bike, and some hospitable camper is likely to suggest sharing his campsite.

Arriving early also gives you time to relax.

One of Oregon's many bikeways is this paved trail in the Champoeg State Park beside the Willamette River. OREGON DEPARTMENT OF TRANSPORTATION PHOTO.

You can unload your bicycle and set up your tent while there is light to see what you are doing. You can go for water, find the wash house, and collect firewood, if it is that kind of campground. You can also prepare your meal and have the camp tidy and ready for the night well before darkness arrives. This is good planning because you probably will not carry a light, at least not one of much power, in your camping outfit, since the light adds weight. The chances are that by nighttime you will be ready for early retirement anyhow.

Where you have a choice of campsites, look the campground over and make a careful selection. Your decision could have much to do with getting a good night's sleep. Try for a camping spot away from the highway and the camp roads. Otherwise you may be disturbed by vehicle traffic. Select a tenting spot that is on higher ground. This usually means a drier place and may also put you where there is a cooling breeze. Lower areas may be near ponds, sloughs or ditches where mosquitoes hold conventions.

Also pick a spot where trees or other obstructions will keep vehicles well away from your tent or your bicycle.

A level tent site is important because most of us sleep uncomfortably on a slope, waking up throughout the night and crawling back uphill. I like camping in pine woods whenever possible. Often this gives your bed a basic pine-needle mattress as a beginning. Besides, the pine woods have a fresh smell—clean and sharp, the way the outdoors should be.

Also, don't choose campsites too near toilets, water pumps or faucets, or even spaces located on a main trail to these facilities. Otherwise the traffic outside your tent may disturb you through much of the night.

Camping groups are to be avoided unless you like amateur singing and guitar strumming long after the road-weary bicycler might normally be asleep. I once found myself camped too near a large Scout troop. I arrived during the dinner hour and the woods were deceptively quiet. After their meal, however, the troop divided into two armies that attacked and retreated back and forth outside my tent through much of the night.

In addition to federally owned lands, numerous states have systems of state parks and forests with campgrounds. More likely than not, a stop in a designated campground requires paying a camping fee. This is often not so for federal lands.

Advantages of regular campgrounds are that these usually have toilets and a source of water, and sometimes even showers or swimming facilities.

Bicycle campers seldom carry bulky campground guides with them, but rely on map information or descriptions they gather from other campers and cyclists along the way. A freewheeling non-plan may work, if you are traveling through areas where much of the land is publicly owned, as it is in some Western states.

There are still places in this country where the traveler and sportsman is welcome to camp outside designated campgrounds. Through much of the National Forest lands, as well as on lands managed by the U. S. Bureau of Land Management, this is often the case. These lands cover millions of acres. You may be traveling through these sprawling federal holdings far from the nearest town, and if you travel with a complete outfit, you can camp where night overtakes you. For those psychologically adjusted to staying alone in wild places, these stops can become pleasant, often unforgettable, memories.

There are, however, a number of points to remember if you make camp outside regular campgrounds. First, be certain that your camp does not violate any current rule. National Forest lands are sometimes closed to camping during seasons when serious fire hazards exist. Signs at the entrance to the forest will often give the traveler such information.

Remember, too, that away from campgrounds you may not have a ready source of safe water. Usually there are no toilets, although you may come across a picnic area where facilities are provided and camping is permissible.

Before choosing a spot for your tent, check the trees. Do not pitch your tent beneath a dead branch that might come down on you in a windstorm. Don't pitch your tent beneath a tree that towers above those around it or stands alone, because such dominant trees attract lightning. Avoid making camp on the flood plain of a river or creek that might become the scene of a flash flood in heavy rains.

When camping away from designated campgrounds, be careful about leaving the area as clean as you found it. This is even more important in such places than in regular camping places, because there is no clean-up crew. There is a growing fraternity of sensitive outdoor people who practice low-impact camping. These are the campers who leave areas so unchanged by their visit that nobody can tell that they have been there. With millions of people traveling in remote places, this low-impact camping is of increasing importance. Natural processes can heal some of the wounds we make on forest, field and desert, but this healing process may require years. Here are some of the ways a camper can stop for a night, then travel on without leaving his mark on the land.

Rocks should not be moved unless they are put back where they were. Fires should not be built against rocks because they blacken them with smoke and soot that will not come off. Only dead and fallen trees should be taken for firewood. Charred firewood lying around is irrefutable evidence that you were on the scene. When you are absolutely certain the fire is out (the ashes feel cool to your hand) bury the ashes. Hot embers, when buried, may set organic material in the soil on fire or start roots burning, creating a fire that flares up long after you have gone.

Streams are more easily abused than we realize. Wash water should not be thrown into a stream. Even bathing with soap pollutes the water for fish and other wildlife as well as for people who might use the water downstream. Instead of disposing of wash water in the creek, put it into the latrine you are going to fill and cover.

Vary your routes between the parts of your campsite to avoid making paths within your camping area. Paths are evidence that people were here and, once started, may grow and detract from the wild nature of the place.

Some things are obvious. Trees should not be cut or hacked. Hangers for clothes, lanterns or kitchen equipment should not be left behind. The fire hazard away from designated campgrounds can be a greater threat to forest and grasslands than it is in established camping areas.

Low-impact camping is a technique whose time has come. Those who practice it feel good about leaving a campground in a condition so unchanged that even a skilled woodsman might have trouble telling that any bicycler stopped in this wild and beautiful place.

THE FEDERAL LANDS

Much of America, especially in the Western states, is still held by the federal government for all of the people, and on these lands there is unlimited opportunity for new outdoor experiences. The public lands are administered by several agencies within the executive branch of the government. Some of them have regional offices which offer assistance to bicyclists and others using the outdoors. Good highway maps often show where the public lands are along your route.

U. S. FOREST SERVICE

The U. S. Forest Service, a branch of the Department of Agriculture, manages our 154 national forests located in 41 states and Puerto Rico. Although timber production is a major purpose of these lands, it is by no means their only use. The Forest Service invites the public to use the forests for camping, fishing, hunting, hiking and exploring. It operates hundreds of public campgrounds, often in country as beautiful as you will find anywhere. In addition, campers are free to set up their tents wherever they choose on many national forests.

You recognize national forests by the big roadside signs the Forest Service erects. Through parts of the West much of your bike route may run through these lands, which are home, in some seasons, to most kinds of big game found in North America; it is not unusual to see elk, deer and bear in many of the forests in Western states.

Individual forests have their own headquarters where visitors are welcome to stop and pick up information on the land, roads, wildlife, fishing and camping.

The Forest Service is also responsible for the 19 national grasslands. These prairie lands are found mostly through the Great Plains states. Although they are utilized primarily for grazing, the government is giving increasing attention to their recreational use.

If you want information on a specific area write: Regional Office, U. S. Forest Service, at the appropriate address in the following list for the region in which you are especially interested:

Northern—Federal Bldg., Missoula, MO 59807
Rocky Mountain—11177 W. 8th Ave., P.O. Box 25127, Lakewood, CO 80225
Southwestern—517 Gold Ave. SW, Albuquerque, NM 87102
Intermountain—324 25th Street, Ogden, UT 84401
California—630 Sansome St., San Francisco, CA 94111
Pacific Northwest—319 SW Pine St., P.O. Box 3623, Portland, OR 97208
Southern—1720 Peachtree Rd., Atlanta, GA 30309
Eastern—633 W. Wisconsin Ave., Milwaukee, WI 53203

NATIONAL WILDLIFE REFUGES

In practically every state the federal government has created refuges for native wildlife, ranging from grizzly bears to seaside sparrows. These lands protect endangered species as well as millions of migratory waterfowl and other birds. Lands in this world-famous system of refuges offer perhaps the best of all opportunities to see and photograph wildlife. Although they are, first of all, for the protection of wildlife, some National Wildlife Refuges have campgrounds open to the public. Among these are the Aransas National Wildlife Refuge on the Gulf Coast of Texas, where campers may see whooping cranes during the winter months; the Wichita Mountains National Wildlife Refuge in Oklahoma, where campers live among wild turkeys, prairie dogs, bison and longhorn cattle; and Red Rock Lakes in Montana where trumpeters—the world's biggest swans—live.

Roadside signs marking national wildlife refuge boundaries are often spotted by touring bicyclists. The refuge headquarters, which may be several miles down a side road, will have free circulars and bird lists, and often maps of the best roads to pedal if you're looking for wildlife.

If you want additional details on the wildlife refuges, write National Wildlife Refuge System, U. S. Fish and Wildlife Service, Department of the Interior, Washington, DC 20240.

BUREAU OF LAND MANAGEMENT

This federal bureau manages 60 per cent of all federally owned lands, mainly in the Western states, including Alaska. These are lands managed for numerous uses, including recreation. BLM land is generally open to camping and hiking, as well as fishing and hunting, within the framework of state laws. For information on these public lands, write Office of Public Affairs, U. S. Bureau of Land Management, Department of the Interior, Washington, DC 20240.

14.

THE RACERS

Ask most Americans what the world's most popular sport is and they might or might not know it is soccer. Ask them to name the second most popular sport worldwide and most are going to fail your quiz. In this country of baseball, basketball and football, we are just not conditioned to the fact that bicycle racing is in the second spot. But it is, and if you lived in Europe this would be much easier to understand. In some parts of the world, outstanding bicycle racers achieve national hero status. Eddy Merckx is a name remembered as widely in Belgium as Tom Seaver, Pete Rose or Reggie Jackson in the United States. What did Eddy Merckx do to become famous? He displayed astounding skill and stamina in bicycle races. He is best known as the five-time winner of the world's most prestigious bicycle race—the 2,500-mile Tour de France. His racing also made him a millionaire.

In the United States, racing is staging a remarkable comeback. Yes, a comeback, since before the advent of the automobile, bicycle racing was big-time here, as it was in Europe. In the early days of this century an important bicycle race would draw a crowd of 30,000. All across America, more than a hundred bicycle racetracks —known as velodromes—were doing a peak business.

There were other races, too, wherever a few professionals or amateurs could be brought together. From the schoolyards to the fanciest professional tracks, bicycle races were important elements of the American scene.

Interests change, however, and bicycles gave way to roaring motors and scraping metal. In a few generations, Americans forgot what it was like to concentrate on the racing bicycle riders who speed over the course, outwitting and outpedaling their competitors.

Although this situation is changing once again, many wonder what the racers gain from their brand of pedaling. One serious racer, who graduated to racing from bicycle touring, once told me, "I don't have time to ride for pleasure anymore." Others may hear the birds and smell the flowers, but the racer puts his or her head down and pedals like a demon. What in the world are they chasing? Maybe a non-racer can never know. The winner may be awarded little more than a belt buckle. But the satisfaction is there, the sense of accomplishment that comes with drawing on his own body for the power needed to win a race, or to finish a difficult run. For some there is also the sound of the cheering and, in big races, perhaps the banking of the prize.

There are many kinds of racing, and new variations seem to come along frequently. Some lead competitors across mountainous courses, on trails marked through swamps and marshes, or simply around a city block. But most races can be classified in one of two groups—track or road.

Track races are conducted at velodromes, oval-shaped tracks banked so riders can take the turns faster. These tracks may vary in length from 250 to 440 meters. The length of the regulation Olympic track is currently 333.33 meters. The shorter the velodrome track, the steeper its banks. Some are banked to 40 degrees, and riders speeding around them at speeds between 40 and 50 miles an hour appear to be hanging to the sides. These tracks may be made of wood, clay, concrete or asphalt. Velodromes can serve for other recreational activities also, an important consideration for cities or communities thinking of building a bicycle racing center. The infield can be flooded for a winter skating rink, or can provide space for soccer or football games.

The idea of building new velodromes was given a major boost in 1967 when Bob Rodale of Emmaus, Pennsylvania, went to Winnipeg, Manitoba, to compete in the skeet shooting events of the Pan Am Games. Rodale's father was a noted advocate of organic gardening who founded two national magazines, *Organic Gardening and Farming* and *Prevention,* which Bob Rodale publishes today along with *Bicycling.* Rodale is a strong advocate of health foods, and of exercise, including bicycling. While in Winnipeg, he witnessed a bicycle race in a velodrome. It was a new and exciting experience for him. In addition to the courage, skill and strength of the racers speeding around the track, Rodale observed the spectators and their high excitement in watching the bicycle racing. He went home inspired to build such a track in Pennsylvania.

Rodale's velodrome at Trexlertown, Pennsylvania, is one of the finest anywhere. The track is 333 meters, and banked as perfectly for racing as engineers could make it. With expert management, the Trexlertown International Velodrome began to attract racers—and nationwide attention. This set other communities and promoters to planning new velodromes of their own.

Bicycles used for racing on these tracks have fixed gears and are not equipped with derailleurs or brakes. The riders cannot coast on them, because as long as the wheels are turning, the pedals go around. These are bikes built for racing—full time at full speed.

On the other hand, bicycles used for road racing are usually ten-speed machines equipped with brakes and derailleurs. Typically, all participants in these races start out at the same time with a single aim—to see who is the first one across the finish line. By contrast, there are time-trial races in which racers are started individually and race against the clock. The one who rides the distance in the best time wins. This kind of race is less exciting for both observer and rider than the massed-start race.

Road races can vary with the roads available and the ideas of those who lay out the course. These races, known among bicyclers as "criteriums," may be around the block or through a town. The racers make a specified number of laps around the course, which is usually less than a mile long. Spectators watch the riders go past, then wait a few minutes for the next lap and watch them again. In this way they see who is in front on each lap, and with experience, begin to understand the strategy of the racers as they work and maneuver for positions.

Often the idea is to follow a pack of bicycles, then toward the end try to leave them behind by sprinting. By letting others serve as windbreaks, the rider conserves energy. But this does not mean there is time to relax. The cyclist is thinking constantly and planning all the time, because at the right moment he or she must be able to break out and try to move ahead. A strong rider, of course, can sprint out in front in the beginning and lead the pack for the whole race.

Criteriums are held in dozens of communities across the country every year. Some draw top riders. Among the best known of these races are those held annually at Somerville, New Jersey; Nevada City, California; Kettering, Ohio; Indianapolis, Indiana; and Los Gatos, California. Some riders travel from one to another on the circuit.

Trying to get into racing at this level is a demanding challenge. The training calls for more physical conditioning and attention to diet than most of us would care to give. There is always the possibility that, regardless of the work and sacrifice, you will not become a competitive racer. The winners have a single-mindedness that keeps them thinking about little except bicycle racing. They learn to concentrate on every element of the race that might make a fractional difference. They are not riding for the sheer pleasure of being outdoors. If you want to get into racing, and have the drive to win, inquire around to see how others began. Write to the Amateur Bicycle League of America to learn the name of the official nearest you.

THE RACERS   125

Successful racing cyclists follow rigid training programs and keep their highly specialized bicycles in perfect condition. BICYCLE MANUFACTURERS ASSOCIATION OF AMERICA, INC., PHOTO.

Racers ride behind each other, allowing the rider in front to break the wind so that the others can save their energy until the opportunity to surge ahead presents itself. BICYCLE MANUFACTURERS ASSOCIATION OF AMERICA, INC., PHOTO.

John Marino in training for his first record-breaking cross-country ride from Santa Monica's City Hall to New York's City Hall, which he completed in thirteen days, one hour and twenty minutes. Marino went on to break his own record in 1980 with a time of twelve days, three hours and thirty-one minutes. CYCLES PEUGEOT.

BMX races are held on special tracks in a growing number of communities throughout the country. In this race at Bakersfield, California, riders are in the fourteen-year-old class. PANDA BIKE COMPANY PHOTO.

THE RACERS

Each summer the blue-gray slopes of the Rocky Mountains become the backdrop for a week-long event that draws top riders from several countries. They come to Boulder, Colorado, to participate in the Red Zinger Bicycle Classic. Each day has its riding events. Races are over mountain roads winding up and down slopes between elevations of 6,000 and 12,500 feet. The Zinger is a grueling race, rich in color and prestige.

On the other hand, if you want to sample bicycle racing without committing yourself so completely, there is a way. "Open" racing allows riders to race in less competitive company than you will find at the big races. In these open races, the rider can begin to see whether or not he or she likes racing and can also have the opportunity to win a trophy or a belt buckle. There are separate races for riders of different ages and abilities.

Open racing is most widespread in Southern California, but cyclists in other areas who want to organize similar events can obtain details from the Open Bicycle Racing Association, 101 N. Citrus, Corvina, CA 91723, by including a stamped, self-addressed envelope with a letter.

Owners of BMX models also have special racing events, which are increasing in number across the country. The early Evel Knievel approach to riding these rugged little bikes has, in many places, given way to organized events that offer prizes as well as status to young riders. Outdoor tracks for BMX events are easily designed and built. These events, held on ¼-mile or ⅛-mile tracks, draw riders from the ages of five to nineteen; riders compete against others of comparable age, skill and experience. Inevitably, cash prizes began to enter the picture and professional BMX riders became part of the bicycle racing world.

One organization that sanctions BMX events is the National Bicycle Association. To compete in any sanctioned BMX event the rider is required to have certain safety equipment. Bars and posts are padded to protect the rider in case of accidents, and all riders must wear helmets and gloves. On these tracks speeds above 13 or 14 miles per hour are unusual, so serious accidents are rare.

If you want to read a book on racing, get a copy of *American Bicycle Racing* at your local library or order one directly from the publisher, Rodale Press, Inc., Emmaus, PA.

Here are some organizations that can supply further information on bicycle racing:

Amateur Bicycle League of America
Box 669 Wall Street Station
New York, NY 10005

Open Bicycle Racing Association
101 N. Citrus
Covina, CA 91723

United States Cycling Federation, Inc.
P.O. Box 480
East Detroit, MI 48121

15.

THE BICYCLE COMMUTER

Although bicycles in the United States are ridden for the sheer pleasure of it by people of all ages, these machines also carry people to work, to school and on errands. Many consider the bicycle to be the vehicle of the future, thanks to rising fuel prices, traffic congestion and mounting pollution levels. To see what a heavy bicycle population looks like we can observe European and Asian cities. Closer to home, the outstanding example of a genuine bicycling city is Davis, California. Davis, a city of 27,000 people, has 20,000 working bicycles. An estimated one-third of the movement of people around Davis is by bicycle.

One reason for this is that Davis is the home of one of the University of California's seven campuses. Student riders, commuting between classes, make up much of the traffic. Others commute to their jobs. Added to these are women going shopping and men running errands. In this atmosphere people begin to think "bicycle" instead of picking up the car keys when they have only a few miles to go.

According to one official report, "Probably the most significant element in maintaining the cycle as a viable form of transportation has been the attitude of Davis residents and city officials and the provisions they have made to insure cycles are not crowded off the streets by automobile traffic."

Since 1966 Davis has purposely engineered facilities for the safety and convenience of bicycle riders. Davis streets were marked off with lanes designated exclusively for bicycles. Some streets were closed to motor vehicles. Greenbelt trails were built. Special parking facilities for bicycles were increased, and officials studied traffic patterns to learn how the bicycles could be moved with maximum safety and efficiency. Where bicycle commuters are common, motorists become accustomed to them and learn to accept the presence of the two-wheelers. People elsewhere constantly relate stories of vengeful drivers or ignorant motorists who turn in front of them or try to run them off the road. "But I simply don't experience this," says a university official who is also a cyclist. "No one hassles me."

What bicyclists are proving in Davis is that the bicycle is a highly satisfactory form of transportation for commuters. Bicycle commuter traffic is increasing in other American cities, but on a smaller scale. Wherever the bicycle is becoming an important part of the city's commuter picture, the trend is led by bicycle riders, not by city officials. Were cities to take the lead, especially in developing safer bicycle routes, commuting by bike would grow still faster. There are excellent arguments in favor of the bicycle as a means of maneuvering through crowded traffic. Careful studies have shown that commuters who work in downtown Washington, D.C., negotiate the traffic to and from work as quickly by bicycle as by automobile during the rush hours. Besides, fourteen bicycles can park in the space taken by a single automobile. In addition, the riders maintain their health and hold down travel costs while adding nothing to the pollution level.

Thousands of bicycles follow special traffic patterns on the campuses of the University of California. UNIVERSITY OF CALIFORNIA PHOTO.

Tests show that bicycle commuters in normal rush hour traffic average speeds almost as good as those of motorists driving the same routes.
U. S. DEPARTMENT OF TRANSPORTATION PHOTO, JAMES CARROLL.

THE BICYCLE COMMUTER

Another, perhaps more typical city with a growing population of bicycle commuters is Boulder, Colorado. Riders in Boulder receive the same treatment as automobile drivers, which means that they are also subject to penalties for infractions of traffic regulations. "While there are bike lanes and paths to a certain extent," reports one commuter there, "I seldom use them, since I find streets much faster—and safer." Statistics collected by a leading Boulder bike shop show four times as many accidents on bike paths, which are used indiscriminately by pedestrians, roller skaters, skateboarders and people with pushcarts.

Another Boulder bike commuter says, "I find that by being very convincing about my right to use the street, and *very* conscious of what the traffic is doing around me at any moment, I succeed in going everywhere that cars do, and sometimes at the same speed."

One federal worker I interviewed in his office in downtown Washington said, at the end of the day, "Wait a minute. I'll ride down with you on the elevator." He went into the adjoining room and returned pushing his ten-speed. The first elevator was crowded with people who did not have their bicycles, so we waited for the next one. "I take the bike up with me," he explained, "because it's safer. I've been riding to work for eight years because, everything considered, it is simpler than getting around in a car." Not everyone, of course, can solve the storage problem by taking a bicycle into the office during the day.

One commuter who proved, at least to his own satisfaction, that the bicycle is the machine to get city workers around easily was Thomas R. Reid III, who moved from his teaching job at Johns Hopkins University to work for the government in Washington. Reid decided early in his stay in the capital city that his bicycle offered the easiest form of transportation. Some co-workers, however, questioned his belief that the bike is faster than driving an automobile. Reid, seeking an answer to the question, set up a race. He planned to time his trip against that of two friends covering the same route in different vehicles. One was to ride the city bus, the other would drive his Porsche. The finish line was the District Building, where they worked.

While lines of cars waited at traffic lights, the bicyclist moved forward and crossed the intersection with the first of the traffic. While the city bus stopped for passengers and other traffic, the bicycle kept moving. Reid arrived at work and looked around for his friends. The Porsche made somewhat better time than the bus, but the driver parked illegally, then dashed across the street to the finish line. Reid, who had already been there for three minutes, proved his point.

This contest did not go unnoticed around Washington. Reid's race helped impress on officials the value of a better system of bicycle trails around the city. Soon special bicycle routes were marked through the center of Washington,

The bicycle is more convenient than the car and, for short trips, frequently faster and more invigorating. It does not increase noise or air pollution levels and is highly energy-efficient. BICYCLE MANUFACTURERS ASSOCIATION OF AMERICA, INC., PHOTO.

leading into Federal Triangle, where thousands of workers converge each day, heading for their government jobs. In addition, a path for bike commuters was planned through Washington's sprawling Rock Creek Park and certain streets were closed to Sunday traffic to make them safer for bicycling. Increasingly, government buildings are being equipped with bicycle racks where riders can lock up their bikes while at work.

In some areas, commercial bicycle lockers have been installed, and other improvements are in the works. Some cities now operate buses with bicycle racks.

A bicycling park ranger leads a family group through Rock Creek Park, Washington, D.C. NATIONAL PARK SERVICE PHOTO.

For short-distance commuting requiring maneuvering in heavy traffic and on relatively level terrain, three- or five-speed bicycles with flat handlebars are often preferable to ten-speeds with turned-down handlebars. U. S. DEPARTMENT OF TRANSPORTATION PHOTO, JAMES CARROLL.

ARE YOU READY FOR COMMUTING?

The first time you ride your bicycle to work through heavy traffic you may be under considerable stress. There is an uneasiness in all of us about tackling new and potentially hazardous situations, especially when we are competing for limited space with many other people. When you begin commuting, you may sense this pressure as you maneuver through traffic. But confidence builds with experience. The commuter knows that he or she has as much right out there on the street as anybody, and that the mode of travel is a matter of individual choice. Your adjustment to commuting by bicycle will probably be easier than you anticipate.

Your safety depends on your ability to concentrate. You should be aware all the time of traffic conditions around you. Potential hazards are best anticipated in advance, allowing you to circumvent the problems. Know your rights and remember that most motorists do not resent the bicyclist who maintains a steady course and who does not make sudden or erratic changes.

As you change over to bicycle commuting, the inclination will be to ride the same routes traveled by car. This is the familiar routing, but it may not be the best way to go on your two-wheeler. Find the most satisfactory bicycle route by studying city maps and exploring streets by bicycle. There may be shortcuts suitable for bicycles but not for cars. These distance-savers may lead through parks where there is the added bonus of pleasant surroundings. Narrow side streets that take you off the heavily traveled arteries may be available, and these deserve to be checked out. A test ride will soon tell you whether or not the pavement is too rough for your safety and comfort or if there are other disadvantages, such as vicious dogs.

These exploratory trips between home and office or factory can be checked out on weekends when you are out riding for pleasure, but the real test comes on workdays, when you are on a schedule.

Whatever the route, allow yourself extra time until your commuting settles down into a regular pattern. With experience, you will know to the minute the time required to travel between home and work, and how much extra time to allow in foul weather. "Traveling the same route at the same time every day," one bicycle commuter told me, "you meet the same motorists and they become accustomed to sharing the road with you."

A vital part of the preliminary planning is finding parking for your bicycle during the day. Before commuting that first time, know where you can leave the bike. Check with other riders who work where you do. If a lack of bicycle parking keeps workers from riding to work, the employer might be willing to establish a bicycle parking area. Approach officials on the subject and find out.

The serious commuter faces occasional problems coping with bad weather. Cold weather calls for garments that will conserve body heat and break the force of the wind. Wet days can be met with rain gear and lightweight fenders. Helmets are always good safety equipment. Consider wearing layers of clothes so you can peel off a sweater or jacket as the need arises. Each person's situation varies somewhat from that of other riders, and you must work out your solution to fit your needs.

There may be days in midwinter when you are pedaling home in darkness or near darkness. There may also be especially dark, cloudy days when visibility is poor. These circumstances require lights, front and back. Get a high-quality set of lights on which you can depend. Your bicycle shop can help on this.

Adequate lighting is serious business for most commuters—perhaps even the key to survival. One who solved this problem was Pete Kutschenreuter, formerly president of the League of American Wheelmen, and a determined bicycle commuter. Pete rides the 12½ miles to and from work every day of the year when weather allows. This means about 45 minutes of riding in rush hour traffic. In the evening he often needs lights to help him get home safely. "I use a double-beam motorcycle headlight," he says, "powered by a six-volt rechargeable wet-cell battery. When I get home, I just plug the battery into a charger and a timer turns it off. This is a minimum of trouble. It provides a strong light for about an hour, giving me extra time for the trip if I need it. People think I'm on a motorcycle."

In addition, Pete has a flashing yellow strobe light on the back, as well as the regular red tail lamp. These, plus all the regulation reflectors and a few extra ones, give motorists little excuse for not seeing him and his bicycle.

The extras you carry may call for a handlebar bag. If you need a change of clothing, you may want to add a pack to the rear carrier. Many commuters carry a lunch, briefcase or both. Experiment in attaching these to your rear carrier with elastic stretch cords. Whatever method you use, be certain the items you carry are fastened down so they will not slip during the trip and are protected from water.

Depending on how far you travel and how hard you must pedal, you may need to change clothes and shower after arriving at work. If there are no facilities for this available, you can adjust your pace to keep from working up a sweat. If you are going to shower and change, you will have to carry additional clothing and pay more attention to packing for the daily trip. At the very least, you may need extra shoes and socks, especially on rainy days. A poncho can keep other parts of you dry most of the time.

Commuting bicyclists, even those who don't

anticipate trouble with their bikes, should give thought to what they will do in case of a flat tire, broken gear cable or broken chain. A foresighted rider will carry an extra tube plus the tools needed to make the change. You will also want wrenches that permit you to tighten handlebars or saddle. Some commuters make a mental note of the location of bicycle repair shops along their routes.

The bicycle is not the only thing that must be in shape for successful commuting. The rider may tire, especially in the beginning. Gradual conditioning can put you in shape and daily commuting will toughen your body and maintain your physical ability.

Commuters sometimes become enthusiastic promoters of the bicycle as a means for getting to and from work. Sally With of Boulder, Colorado, says, "I very much enjoy being fully dependent on my bicycle for transportation, even though we live in a cabin about five miles up Boulder Canyon. I fly down to work each morning, and I return—at considerably slower speed—each evening." She equips her bike with panniers in which she carries ". . . tools, various changes of clothing, rain gear, food, books, a filing system for important papers, etc." She rides a Bianchi with Suntour derailleurs, Weinmann wheels, rims and brakes, and a Blackburn rack. She has attached reflectors to most available spaces on the bicycle and has also added triangles of yellow reflector tape on the backs of the yellow panniers.

"We have carried many loads up the canyon," she adds, "including large amounts of groceries, logs we find on the road, a stereo turntable and a sewing machine. Those who prepare their bodies and their machines now," she adds, "will be in the best shape for getting around after the coming demise of the petrochemical society."

Commuters can improve conditions for themselves if they play a role in the political process. There is much to be accomplished by citizen action—not placard-carrying marches on City Hall, but reasoned discussions with planners and leaders. Numerous changes that would improve life for bicycle commuters can be brought about in this way. A big need exists for safer storage facilities at subway stations, commuter rail depots and bus terminals. At present few office buildings or factories provide good storage conditions for bicycles. Commuter trains themselves should

Bicycle rack, of tubular steel construction, holds three bikes on each side. TROXEL MANUFACTURING COMPANY PHOTO.

have bicycle racks so that commuters can take their bikes with them to ride in the city. This is common in European cities.

Bicyclists also need to work for better bicycle paths or bikeways. Most cities, unlike Davis, California, have made only rudimentary progress in this direction, but there has been an awakening of interest. Recently even New York has tested the idea of marking off narrow bike lanes in mid-Manhattan. If your city has not begun such a program, the reason may lie in the fact that nobody has taken the problem to the city leaders.

Riders themselves should play a role in speeding the creation of bicycle commuter facilities. Group action accomplishes more than individual effort. Urge your bicycle club, civic group, or employee organization to undertake a campaign to improve facilities for bicycle commuters. Once a group begins to study the possibilities and appoints committees to take its message to the powers that be, it has taken the first step in replacing some of those gasoline guzzlers with nonpolluting vehicles. It's a worthy goal.

16.
YOUR BICYCLE AND YOUR HEALTH

Today we sit in our school or office hour after hour, or we spend eight hours a day in a specialized factory job that employs the same muscles constantly. We sit inactively when traveling in cars and spend a great deal of time sitting in front of the television. Meanwhile, we eat rich foods and tell ourselves that we are going to start dieting. Doctors everywhere, even those who do not follow their own advice, agree that regular sustained exercise can prolong our lives and goes a long way toward correcting the problems inherited with our modern life-style. Although jogging is generally conceded to be a slightly better all-around exercise than bicycling, I find jogging a boring activity compared with bicycling. It is said that the way to tell the difference between a bicyclist and a jogger is that the bicyclist is smiling.

A bicycle allows the rider to exercise while seeing the countryside. After a day of sedentary work the physical exertion eases tensions and relaxes muscles. It also strengthens the heart and builds the efficiency of the lungs.

If there is any question in your mind about your physical condition, let your doctor in on your plans. Have a complete physical checkup before engaging in any serious or prolonged bicycling. An annual physical is sound practice for anyone over thirty-five in any case, whether you think you need it or not.

No form of vigorous exercise should be adopted without building up to it gradually. The path to real physical difficulties, including the possibility of heart attacks, say the doctors, is for a person in poor condition to jump on a bike and ride off on a prolonged jaunt, forcing himself to go farther and faster than he should at this stage. Start by riding a few miles, or even less, a day. Keep at it. Ride every day if you can, and if conditions prohibit this, try to ride at least three or four times a week. Gradually increase the distance covered. Your body will tell you how much you can ride comfortably.

Professional athletes understand the importance of warming up before they begin vigorous physical exercise. Cyclists should take the same approach. Start out on your daily ride at an easy pace and use lower gears until your body loosens up and you are ready for more demanding pedaling. If the session is going to be good exercise, however, the rider has to work hard once the initial warm-up period is over. Only by exerting yourself will you increase your strength and stamina.

Once you complete a vigorous session of bicycling, finish up with a cooling-down period. The last couple of miles of your ride should be an easy pedaling time again, just as the first few miles were. You should be able to work yourself into an exercise program that can reduce your weight (if that's a problem), lift your spirits and keep a spring in your step.

Rental bicycles are often available to vacationers who want healthful exercise and the pleasure of exploring at a leisurely pace. BICYCLE MANUFACTURERS ASSOCIATION OF AMERICA, INC., PHOTO.

WHAT ABOUT AIR POLLUTION?

As bicycle use soared in recent years and cyclists increasingly shared highways and commuter routes with automobiles, an important question was posed: bicyclists, doctors and government officials began asking if motor vehicle exhaust might be poisoning the air to a level that threatens the cyclist's health. The U. S. Department of Transportation (DOT), which includes a section working to promote bicycle use, decided to get a handle on this pollution question by conducting a research project. The report based on this research came from DOT late in 1977. Bicyclers everywhere might well be interested. The report is titled "A Study of the Health Effects of Bicycling in an Urban Atmosphere."

Technicians and medical specialists selected ten healthy male cyclists to participate in the test. They also selected a control group whose members were to travel the routes in automobiles at the same time. In this way, both the bicyclists and automobile drivers could be tested after each run to compare the effects of air pollution.

The test routes covered a variety of streets and commuter routes in and around Washington, D.C., which has a growing community of people using bicycles to get to and from work. The routes included 30- and 60-minute trips, to give a variety of conditions in peak traffic hours.

As each rider finished a run, he was checked for a series of eleven signs and symptoms that could reveal the effects of air pollution on his health. Before and after each run, participants were tested for blood levels of carboxyhemoglobin (CO), carbon monoxide and a wide variety of other pollutants. The report began with a statement saying that "no major adverse short-term health effects were noted while bicycling or driving in levels of pollution and thermal stress during the testing period." Furthermore, the study found that the motorists in the control group and the bicyclists built up similar levels of CO during the test runs.

The DOT study did not, however, close the subject or give a blanket guarantee on safety from air pollution for all who want to get out there and pedal in heavy traffic. It pointed out that additional studies are needed in other cities and that studies are also needed to determine whether or not it would be better to separate bicycle trails some distance from automobile trails to reduce the air pollution danger for cyclists. There is test evidence to indicate that bicyclists are far less likely to suffer ill effects from lead, sulfur oxides, nitrogen oxides and carbon monoxide when the trails are separated by even 30 to 50 feet. These are considerations to be taken seriously.

Before you relax too much on the basis of the DOT findings, remember also that the test subjects were selected for their sound health. The use of less robust subjects might have resulted in less comforting findings. Also, these test riders were nonsmokers. Besides, there are pollutants with which the test did not deal. Personally, I remain skeptical. All those foreign elements in the air cannot be good for us, and the conclusion was that adverse short-term effects were *not noted*. Nobody is saying that breathing the fumes of motor vehicles is harmless.

What the tests indicate is that healthy riders can travel through the streets of Washington, D.C., suffering no more ill effects from air pollution than those driving automobiles. Polluted air is obviously bad for all of us, no matter what we are riding. The human body has not evolved with the ability to cope with the junk we dump into the air and draw into our bodies.

If conditions permit, you are better off doing your pedaling during periods of non-peak traffic and on pathways or trails far from the fume-spouting automobile. Those fumes, under certain circumstances, may do you no harm, but there is no way they are going to benefit you.

ROLLERS FOR EXERCISE

If you and your bike are kept indoors by winter's ice, snow and wind, and you miss those sessions of pedaling, there is a way you can keep in shape as you wait for spring again. You can outfit your basement or recreation room with a

Bicycle Exerciser Kit converts bicycle to exerciser. J.C.I. BICYCLE PRODUCTS.

set of rollers on which the bike runs in place. Racers often use them to keep in trim the year around.

Rollers are mounted on a framework. The two in back are mounted so that the back wheel of your bike can ride on them. The third one is adjustable, and you center it precisely beneath your bike's front wheel.

Riding on such rollers may take some practice at first. You have to stay upright until you build up enough speed to keep your balance. Once that is accomplished, you should find maintaining your balance no more difficult than when riding the bike outdoors. One secret, at least in the beginning, is not to look down at those whirling rollers. Look out ahead instead, as you do when riding normally. You will need something to steady you as you get on the bike. It is good planning to set up the equipment in a clear space to minimize the hazard if you should tumble off.

What about the boredom factor? This can be reduced by varying the rate of pedaling. Some riders even set up rollers in front of the television and watch their favorite programs while exercising.

POSTSCRIPT

The world of medicine showed heightened interest in bicycling as long-distance cyclist John Marino set new records for crossing the country by bicycle in the late 1970s. In the summer of 1978 Marino, a thirty-year-old physical education teacher, completed the 2,954-mile trans-America trip in a little more than thirteen days, a world record. Riding his ten-speed Peugeot, he averaged 230 miles a day and extended the final day to cover 390 miles in twenty-nine hours of continuous riding.

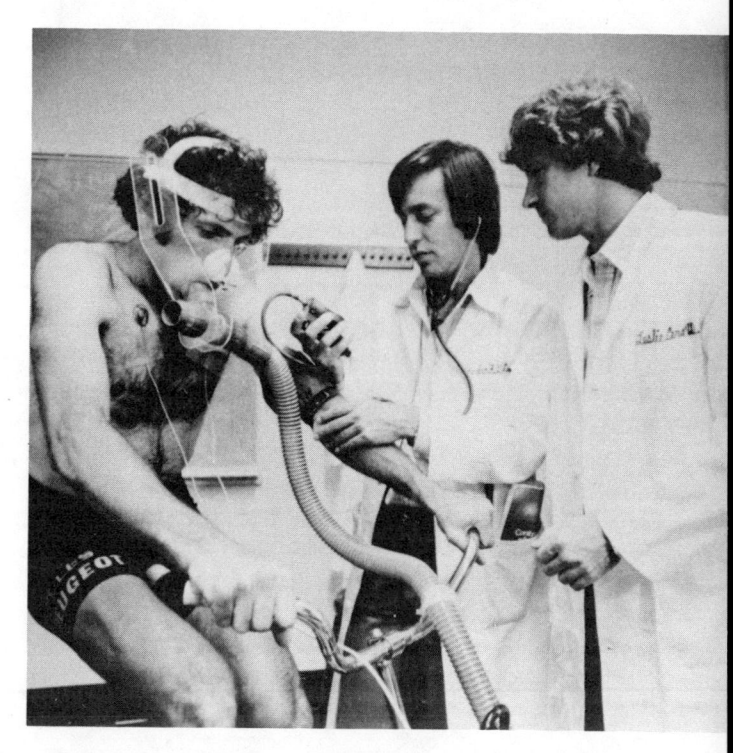

John Marino, trans-American bicycle record holder, has heart and lung functions measured prior to leaving on his cross-country ride. PEUGEOT PHOTO.

This, however, was not good enough for Marino. He was back the following year, intending to ride three thousand miles in twelve and a half days, to beat his own record. His accomplishments were testimony to the ability of the human body and the power of concentration and determination. His riding was closely monitored by a team of medical doctors and technicians. Dr. Charles Kleeman, Director of the Center for Health Enhancement at UCLA, called Marino's record, "staggering." The cyclist's accomplishments, the doctor added, verified the fact that cycling is "Terrific physical exercise."

Marino's diet consisted of grains plus organically grown fruits and vegetables eaten raw, along with distilled water and herbs. What his accomplishments mean for all of us is that we can probably become much better bicycle riders than we are, a realization which should lead to an increase in the use of bicycles and a reduction of our dependence on motor-driven vehicles. Few of us will approach John Marino's riding abilities or physical accomplishments, but his experience indicates that riding can be an important factor in maintaining better physical fitness.

17. RIDE SAFELY

The little blue pickup truck came toward the yield sign at what seemed to me to be excessive speed. The right-of-way was mine, but we were reaching the intersection at the same time. I could see that he expected me to stop and let him go barreling through the "yield" sign. He saw no reason why his souped-up vehicle should give way to a bicycle. As I swerved aside, he clamped down on his brakes and came to a halt beside me.

It is not unusual to become angry when you are scared. I was both. With considerable effort, I refrained from shouting as I pointed out that our vehicles had equal rights, that he was breaking the law by not yielding and that perhaps we should summon a police officer to settle our dispute. The driver suggested that I learn to ride a bike, then, shifting into low gear, he screeched away, leaving me in a blue haze of motor fumes.

Most of us who ride regularly are going to have such an encounter sometime. Bicycle riders always run the risk of confrontations with inconsiderate motor vehicle drivers, especially in communities where bicycles are not common on streets and highways.

This attitude is often most noticeable during the afternoon rush hour when factory shifts are changing. After eight hours cooped up at the same machine or in the same office, the workers are suddenly turned free. Some of them take their frustrations with them and work them off behind the wheel of a car.

Most cyclists classify the automobile as their greatest danger. A car can force you off the road into a ditch. Some drivers seem not to realize how close they crowd bicycles. It is not true that "a miss is as good as a mile." The wind from a vehicle can make a bike swerve. A near collision can so unnerve a rider that he or she loses control. This may put the bike in a ditch or, worse yet, in the path of another automobile. For these reasons some determined riders take their share out of the middle of the traffic lane and calmly let the automobiles stack up behind them, insisting correctly that the bicycle has as much right to a share of the highway as the automobile.

It is one thing to be right, but another to be knocked off your bicycle by a two-ton vehicle. My preference is to ride, if possible, where the cars can pass if there actually is enough room. But going into the gravel is always hazardous, especially on modern lightweight bicycles, and when this is the choice, your best policy is to retain your place in the highway lane and let the car wait until it has room to pass.

In riding around town, automobiles also present a hazard by pulling away from the curb in front of you. When coming up from the rear, I watch the front wheel of any stationary vehicle in front of me if someone is sitting in the driver's seat. The front wheel is often the first part of the car you will see moving. If you are watching, you will have time to slow down or stop.

Another hazard is the driver who swings the door open just in time to catch a passing bicycle. The best defense is to remain constantly at full

Bicycles are considered vehicles and riders are required to comply with all traffic regulations. BICYCLE MANUFACTURERS ASSOCIATION OF AMERICA, INC., PHOTO.

Numerous Florida cities have designated special bicycle routes: Miami has a special system of scenic bicycle trails free of motor traffic. FLORIDA DIVISION OF TOURISM PHOTO.

Young riders should understand traffic laws and their personal responsibility on the road. U. S. DEPARTMENT OF TRANSPORTATION PHOTO, JAMES CARROLL.

alert while bicycling in congested areas. The light weight of your vehicle puts you at a definite disadvantage. Your only real defense is to avoid trouble.

Until such time as the bicycle does become a more accepted part of the traffic pattern, we can anticipate bicycle-automobile conflicts. There are times when these accidents are difficult for bicyclists to understand. Some who have studied the problem believe that either the cyclist is not seen by the motor vehicle drivers or what they see does not register on their minds. Theirs is a big-vehicle world, surrounded by protective steel and transported by a powerful motor.

In addition, the drivers have speed in their favor. A special study done for the city of Davis and the University of California says, "The speed differential in itself causes specific traffic problems as well as producing driver irritation and impatience when delayed by a bike. The combination of greater speed and potential and mass tends to produce a driver arrogance in which the roadway is assumed to inherently belong to the auto, while the bike, as an inferior vehicle, is expected to yield." This brings conflict because the bicyclist wants to maintain momentum and sees no reason to slow or stop frequently at the whim of motor vehicle drivers who are doing no physical work to get themselves from point A to B. The results range from sour looks or obscene gestures to collisions.

Davis, however, because of engineering, law enforcement and driver attitude, has a remarkably low bicycle accident rate. With its more than 20,000 bicycles on the streets, this city experiences only 30 to 35 accidents a year involving bicycles, a rate that many cities of similar size and far fewer bicycles might envy.

The truth, however, is that *bicyclists themselves are responsible for most accidents involving bicycles and motor vehicles.* This aspect of bicycle safety is not one most of us enjoy reading about. But it is still a vital part of the bicycle story. Those in the bicycle industry are sharply aware of the need for riders to work constantly for better safety records, and they spend much time and money promoting safer bicycling.

The record is not good, and the statistics are depressing. In one recent year when there were 55,800 traffic fatalities in the United States, 1,100 of them were bicycle riders. The National Safety Council estimates that there are a million highway injuries a year associated with bicycles. These are injuries serious enough to require medical attention. The fact is, according to research studies, that most bicycle accidents, unless they involve deaths, do not get reported to police departments.

Of the people involved in bicycle accidents, 78 per cent are children. In urban communities, rush hour traffic accounts for a large percentage of the accidents. Frequently the cause is traced to the bicyclist's failure to observe traffic regulations.

In Detroit, investigators checked into the causes of serious collisions involving bicycle riders. Bicyclists coming out of driveways into the paths of automobiles were a big factor. So were those riding into streets from between parked cars. Others entered intersections carelessly, changed directions while riding in front of cars, disobeyed traffic signs, rode on sidewalks, crossed streets in the middle of the block and failed to watch for vehicles coming out of alleys or driveways.

Another study, this one by the American Association for Automotive Medicine, found that bicyclists are less careful to observe traffic regulations than motorists are. In addition, this group mentioned that injured bicyclists are often children not well trained to cope with traffic. They are frequently riding bicycles too large for them, making it difficult to keep the bicycle under control, especially at slow speeds or when stopping. This study plainly said that part of the problem lies in allowing children to ride bicycles that are only scaled-down versions of adult bikes or that have "high-rise" handlebars.

These findings are backed up by a North Carolina study showing that, typically, the rider involved in an accident is a youngster, between ten and fourteen years old, who makes an unexpected entrance into the street from driveway or alley. Furthermore, such accidents often occur on clear, dry days. This North Carolina study also found that fatal accidents frequently occur among older riders touring open country where motor vehicles travel at high speeds. Still another study, this one in Illinois, found that most bicycle accidents occur from May through August, in cities ranging from 10,000 to 100,000 population, and that those involved are most often between the ages of five and fourteen.

Bicycle riders and motor-propelled citizens both must face the fact that the world is becoming increasingly crowded and that there are rules of behavior that will help them prevent conflicts. Bicyclists, unlike motorists, seldom have to pass examinations or obtain licenses to take their vehicles on public thoroughfares. Generally, once a person can comply with the laws of physics and balance a bicycle well enough to keep it upright, he is free to go out there and mix it up. In a few cities riders under twelve may not legally ride on streets, but in most places there is no such restriction. There is rarely any required training program. This may be one reason why young cyclists are seen riding on the wrong side of the road against the oncoming traffic, perhaps wobbling a little, but apparently convinced that they belong there and blissfully unaware that they are breaking the law and endangering their lives. Young beginning riders, however, are not the only ones who ignore stop signs and cut across intersections to keep from slowing down, or fail to give the correct hand signals before changing directions.

There are extensive programs run by a number of concerned agencies to promote safety among bicycle riders. Cincinnati's program may be a typical example of what is being done by the larger cities. During the summer months an officer hitches a bicycle-safety test trailer to his official car and begins the rounds of parks and playgrounds. Bicycle riders are encouraged to bring their machines in for a safety check and a sticker. The officer discusses bicycle safety with these young riders and informs them of out-of-line wheels or other parts that need repairing. In addition, he registers the bike. Then, if it is

Safety measures are best learned by riders who are still young. Teaching bicycle safety should be considered a parental responsibility, not simply a task for schools or police departments. BICYCLE MANUFACTURERS ASSOCIATION OF AMERICA, INC., PHOTO.

stolen, it can be more easily traced. Other cities also have bicycle safety programs, some more and some less effective.

During the school year, many schools conduct demonstrations and review classes on safe bicycle handling. Automobile clubs distribute literature on the subject, and public libraries offer a variety of films on bicycle safety.

In other words, the resources are out there, but essentially bicycle safety training begins within the family. Parents have a major responsibility to see that their children understand the basic rules of safe bicycle riding and practice them.

The first rule is that the bike rider is subject to the same laws that motorists must observe on the public thoroughfares. In addition, bicyclists everywhere may assume that the following rules apply to them:

- The bicyclist must obey the directions of authorized traffic officers.

- Traffic lights and signs of all kinds apply to bicyclists as well as motorists.

- Bicycles should be ridden as close to the right-hand edge of the road as practical. Some bicyclists argue that this encourages motorists to try to squeeze past when traffic is approaching from the other direction and that they have as much right to use the entire lane as a motor vehicle does. Although they have a legal point in this argument, the rule holds that the bicycle should be reasonably close to the right side of the road.

- Bicycles passing vehicles going in the same direction usually, where possible and safe, do so on the right, although passing on the left is legal.

Bicyclists who come to a wildlife crossing should yield the right of way. BICYCLE MANUFACTURERS ASSOCIATION OF AMERICA, INC., PHOTO.

RIDE SAFELY

- Riding against the traffic on a one-way street is illegal.

- Some states and cities prohibit bicycle riding on sidewalks.

- Bicyclists riding on a sidewalk (where legal) must yield the right-of-way to pedestrians.

- When riding a bicycle, travel on the right side of the road, going *with* the traffic—not on the other side, against the traffic, as pedestrians do.

- A bicyclist walking his bicycle must observe the rules for pedestrians. Walk on sidewalks, or on the shoulder on the left side of the road.

- Where there is a usable bicycle path adjacent to the highway, the bicyclist should use that trail, not the roadway.

THE BICYCLE

Some bicycles are not as safe to ride as others. To provide maximum safety the bicycle should be matched to the rider. Young riders often have bikes that are too big for them. Parents buy a too-large bicycle, figuring that the child will grow into it. This means that the time of greatest difficulty in handling the off-size machine comes when the rider is youngest and least experienced. The rider will be far safer if given a bicycle of a size to match his own measurements, then permitted to graduate into a larger bike when the time comes for it. The bicycle that is too big is not easily controlled, and when stopped may fall over because the rider has difficulty putting his or her feet on the ground.

High-rise handlebars make bikes difficult to control by the very nature of their design. They are not safe vehicles on street or roadway and should be restricted to open lots or yards where the rider will not be matched against motorists.

Any bicycle should be inspected at least twice a year to see that it is in top condition. Here are the points that should be regularly inspected:

CHAIN should fit properly, be lightly lubricated and free of damaged links.

PEDALS should be tight and, if heavily worn, replaced.

U. S. DEPARTMENT OF TRANSPORTATION PHOTO.

WHEELS should operate smoothly, be held securely and not wobble.

TIRES should be replaced if worn thin, should not carry embedded foreign materials and should have proper inflation maintained.

HANDLEBARS should be kept tightened and should be adjusted if not comfortable for the rider. Check to see that the stem is deep enough in the head tube.

HANDLE GRIPS should fit snugly or be replaced.

SADDLE should be kept tight and properly adjusted.

BRAKES must apply force equally and all parts should be in good condition.

REFLECTORS should be clean and unbroken.

SPOKES should be kept tight and replaced when broken.

LIGHTS AND HORN should be in good condition and should fit securely.

The commuting bicyclist needs to be a bold and confident rider whose movements are predictable and who makes his changes of direction known to other drivers. U. S. DEPARTMENT OF TRANSPORTATION PHOTO, JAMES CARROLL.

MAINTENANCE FOR SAFETY

There are little things that can make a big difference in how your bicycle operates, and you will recognize these as you become accustomed to carrying out your own maintenance.

You may apply the brakes and find that the instant the brake pad touches the front wheel rim, it sets up an ear-piercing screech. This problem is easily solved. The pad is not hitting the rim flat. Instead, the front edge of the pad is touching the rim first. Simply loosen, adjust and tighten the pad.

Many riders keep their bicycle saddle adjusted at too low a level. It is a common, and mistaken, belief that a rider should be able to straddle the seat of a ten-speed with turned-down handlebars and have the feet flat on the ground. If you can do this, the bike saddle should be raised. If the bike is properly fitted to your size, you should have the feet flat on the ground when straddling the top tube, not the seat. This height calls for a little more care in stopping, but gives much greater comfort and efficient use of energy when riding. A serious rider learns to think about the bicycle each time it is ridden and to take pride in always having the machine in the best possible condition.

NIGHT RIDING

If you plan to ride after dark, reconsider. My advice is to avoid nighttime riding if possible. At times there may seem to be no feasible alternative, such as when you have been held up late in the day by having to repair a bike on the road and have no place to stay short of the next town. Drunk drivers are far more likely to be out at night than during the daylight hours, and the unusual lights and reflectors on a bicycle may confuse the foggy mind.

An example of the tragedy that can stem from this situation occurred in Arizona and was reported in the *L.A.W. Bulletin*. The Central Arizona Bicycle Association was convinced that people should have more experience riding at night. Its members also felt that motorists should learn that bicyclists have the same right to be on the highways at night as they have during daylight hours. They scheduled an "Insomnia Ride" to start at midnight on a Saturday night and extend until dawn. The route extended for 100 km. Twenty-nine minutes after the trip started, a drunk driver ran down and killed one of the riders, then left the scene. Another serious accident happened at 4 A.M. when a second drunk driver struck a young mother who was an experienced bicyclist. She was wearing a helmet and credits it with saving her life. Even so, she spent three weeks in the hospital recovering from a skull fracture, concussion, various broken bones and a disfiguring injury to her face. For weeks she wore a cast on one leg and got around as best she could on crutches.

You might argue that these accidents can happen anytime—daytime included—and you would be right. The chances are greater at night, however—especially Saturday nights and holidays, when there is more than the usual amount of drinking. Even designated bicycle trails, where you will not encounter motor vehicles, hold special hazards after dark if they are used by riders with unlighted bikes, by skateboarders or strolling pedestrians.

REFLECTORS

New bicycles come with approved reflectors, but you may want to add other reflectors for additional visibility. Both manufacturers and government agencies have tested reflectors to learn which provide the greatest measure of safety. The standard system calls for a red reflector on the rear of the vehicle and an amber or clear one on the front. This color combination should then give the approaching motorist an immediate clue as to whether the bicycle is coming toward him or going away.

Also, with proper reflectors, the machine can be identified as a bike from the time it is first spotted. By federal law, new bikes now come with reflectors mounted on the spokes of each wheel. These are neither red nor amber, but clear, because clear reflectors have been found to give visible light reflection four times as bright as similar-size red reflectors.

In addition, the edges of the pedals are a good location for amber reflectors that drivers can easily identify as part of a bicycle.

In addition, some riders add reflectors to frame, fenders and ends of handlebars. These added reflectors should follow the established policy: red on the rear and crystal or clear on those facing the front. Modern reflectors, made of lightweight plastic, add insignificant weight to a bicycle.

You can also select clothing to make yourself more visible on the road. Orange and yellow are highly visible as compared to most other colors. You can purchase reflector tape at your bike shop for application to your helmet or jacket. There are also belts or shoulder straps especially made of these reflective materials.

"For protection," says one Boulder, Colorado, bicycle commuter, "I painted my beautiful red Bianchi a tacky Day-Glo orange, very chintzy, but visible. I have an arrow of reflective tape sewn to the back of my parka, indicating to motorists that they should go around me in the direction in which it points. I have ankle bands of orange reflective tape, a leg light, a back reflector, reflectors on the pedals and warning triangles of reflective tape on the backs of my panniers. I also sewed a strip of reflective tape on the front of my handlebar bag just to be sure I'm seen."

IF FRONT WHEELS LOCK

If the back wheel of your bike should lock tight, the most that could happen is that you drag to a stop. But when the front wheel locks while the bike is moving, the results can be much more serious. Old-time riders of high-wheel bikes knew that one of the supreme hazards they faced was having anything slow down or stop that big wheel over which they were perched. If that happened, they went flying over the top and came to the ground in front of the machine. The same thing occurs in a modified fashion with any modern bicycle. At slow speeds the rider may simply tumble over the handlebars, while at higher speeds he flies out somewhere ahead of the bike, probably tumbling in the process, unable to control which part of the body will take the force of the fall. The results can be fatal.

What causes front-wheel locking? There are several ways this can happen, and every bicyclist should understand them. One might be the front carrier. The carrier itself should cause no hazard if it is tightly mounted, but some riders carry items on it that could catch in the wheel. This might be a garment or the strap of a bag. Book bags draped from handlebars can work their way into the front wheel.

Equipment that can catch in the front wheel and lock it includes reflectors that slip on the spokes, fenders allowed to work loose and a caliper brake that works loose because it is not securely fastened with lock washer and locking nuts. If you want to equip your bicycle with a generator, mount it on the rear wheel for safety.

New bicycles should be checked to see that all parts are securely tightened, especially if the bicycle was not put together by an authorized dealer.

STORM SEWERS

Paved areas collect water and engineers must figure a system for disposing of this surplus. The answer is storm sewers. But grates over openings to these sewers can wreck bicycles. The steel grate over the storm sewer typically has a pattern of long, narrow openings. If these openings are parallel to the road, a bike wheel can drop into one of them, sending the rider over the handlebars and probably wrecking the wheel as well.

If your local streets have storm sewer covers that are a hazard, the problem should be called to the attention of local highway or safety officials. Bicyclists in Loveland, Ohio, obtained permission from the city to paint dangerous sewer grates within city limits a bright yellow—a good club project anywhere these grates present a hazard. Meanwhile, bicyclists must watch out for storm sewer openings.

MAN'S BEST WHAT?

You will not be a bicyclist for long before you realize that some dogs rank near the top on any list of threats to your safety. A friend of mine, an experienced cyclist, says, "I find myself looking at all the places a dog could hide, especially the bushes at the edge of lawns. They like to lurk in such places and wait for the cyclist to get close enough for an attack."

Dog owners who question this should try bicycling. Dogs, even those that normally seem to be no threat, often charge across yards and onto the road to attack bicyclists. They may try to bite into the front tire, or they may hurl themselves into the side of the bicycle as they reach for the rider's moving leg.

This can, and does, cause serious, even fatal, accidents. Where several cyclists are riding together, the dog often singles out the lead machine for its attack, and if it succeeds in knocking the bike over, there may follow a wild collection of tangled bicycles and riders brought down by a single canine.

People have speculated on why dogs attack bicycles. I have my own theory. Domestic dogs trace their ancestry to wolves and perhaps other wild canines. The forerunners of today's pet dogs were predators of the highest order, their survival depending on how well they overpowered weaker creatures. In the world of predators and prey it is often the weak that are singled out for attack. The combination of bicycle and human rider, for some reason, may arouse inherited predatory instincts. The killer drive is triggered and the dog launches an attack against what it senses is a vulnerable target.

In addition, dogs are, by nature, territorial. They defend their territories against all who might threaten their social structure. Reasoning does not come into the picture. If your territory is invaded—attack.

Whether these natural traits of dogs explain their attacks on bicycles or not becomes purely academic to the cyclist trying to protect body and bicycle from the charging canine. Bicyclists have long searched for effective ways to deter vicious dogs.

One of the best is to dismount and keep the bicycle between yourself and the dog. Walk the bike out of his territory, because you can expect the attack to resume the instant you remount to make your escape. If you can stay on your bike and gain speed enough to outdistance the dog, so much the better. This plan is not likely to work with those experienced bike chasers that have learned to quarter the lawn and cut you off at the pass.

The more frightened a rider becomes, the greater the dog's advantage. Show a dog that you have no fear of it and your chances of discouraging the attack improve. There is no law against yelling at a dog, even if its owner is standing in his yard looking at you. Some owners appear to think that if their dog chases a bicycle it is all good clean fun. The law, however, is surely on the side of the rider. There is, incidentally, no relationship between a dog's size and its desire to attack bicycles. Poodles, while less of a threat than a Doberman or a shepherd, can come at you with equal determination and cause a spill.

Bicycle-mounted policemen, such as this one in the nation's capital, are equipped to control traffic. U. S. DEPARTMENT OF TRANSPORTATION PHOTO, JAMES CARROLL.

Bicycle stores often offer equipment especially designed to discourage dogs. One such product is a spray can of chemical that you carry in a clip. Another is a product that gives the dog a discouraging, but harmless, electrical jolt. Those loud freon-powered horns will send some dogs scurrying for shelter.

Some bicyclists carry a switch and try to whack attacking dogs across the nose with it. But if a dog gets this close, you may already be having trouble maintaining your balance, and flailing at a dog only intensifies your risk. Another possibility is to clip onto your bicycle a plastic bottle filled with ammonia and equipped with one of those little Windex-type squirt pumps.

THE ART OF FALLING

Few riders get through life without taking a tumble. Racers know they are going to have bad moments. Tourists and casual riders also hit the ground on occasion. Touring bicyclists seldom know the road ahead and, while this is a large part of cycling's appeal, it can also be a source of unpleasant surprises, especially if the tour leads through hill country.

What do you do if you must fall? There is no way to go down gracefully. All you can hope for is saving yourself as many cuts, scratches and broken parts as possible. The rule is, if you have any control over how you fall, to land on your forearm and roll as a football player might. The rolling will slow you and, although you may get banged up, there is less chance of broken bones than there would be if you crash down on your shoulder. To land on your forearm you will have to get your hands off the handlebars as you come to the ground. And why not? By this time the machine is out of control anyhow. This is the moment you appreciate your helmet and are glad it is securely fastened.

Safe riding becomes a matter of attitude, alertness and a dash of luck. The least of these is luck. Riders can, to a large degree, make their own luck. Those who know how to handle their bikes well, who remain alert and who do not take chances should be in for a long spell of good luck. One bicyclist told me that riding from New York to Boulder, Colorado, she had only one spill. The reason for the sole spill? "I didn't rest enough and I fell asleep while I was pedaling."

18.

THE BIKE STEALERS

Anyone who has been through it can tell you that returning to the parking spot where you left your bicycle and finding it gone leaves an empty and frustrated feeling. This happens every day—many times every day, and in all parts of the country. Bicycle stealing is a big business, and especially in communities where bicycles are abundant, professional thieves are likely to be lurking in the shadows. A South Carolina report estimated that in any given year 1.6 per cent of that state's one million bicycles are stolen. Meanwhile, a comprehensive Davis, California, study tells us that in one year the bicycles stolen in that state represented a $90 million loss.

Bicycle thefts are especially common around apartments and residence halls in university communities, where the thieves have a big choice of machines. Many are taken from shopping centers.

These cases fall into two classes. Often a bicycle is taken because some joker doesn't want to walk all the way across campus or downtown to the store. This brand of thief runs his or her errand, then abandons the "borrowed" bicycle at the destination. Then there are the professionals who make a business of reselling other people's bicycles. They possess bolt cutters, probably stolen, and have a thorough knowledge of various safety devices and how quickly they may be opened or broken. They pick times when owners are sleeping, attending class, out shopping or on the job. They are gone with the bike by the time the owner appears. These bicycle thieves understand that once the bike is taken, the chances of being caught are minimal.

Professional thieves usually pass up the less expensive coaster brake bicycles and the three-speed bikes. They're after the ten-speeds or fifteen-speeds, the more costly the better. The higher resale value makes their risky work more profitable. This accounts for the fact that 90 per cent of the less costly bicycles reported stolen in Davis, California, are soon recovered. They are taken for a ride, then abandoned. But among those who lose ten-speeds in the same city, only 10 per cent can expect to get them back.

If you have never bothered to look for the serial number of your bicycle, or make a record of it, you have missed one step that could help you recover the machine in case it is stolen. If you need to report a stolen bicycle to the police, it is always helpful to give the serial number. Telling the investigating officer, "Well, it's red and it's a ten-speed" gives him too little to go on. Most owners probably have no idea what the serial number of their bicycle is. Manufacturers stamp serial numbers onto their products, but there is no uniform system, and no single location where these numbers are to be found. "But somewhere on the bicycle," says Jim Kucera of Schwinn, "there will be a number, and if you look you'll find it." Record this number in some place where you can always find it easily: in the back of your checkbook, on a special note card in your wallet

THE BIKE STEALERS

or on the wall above your workbench. When paying for a bicycle, note the serial number on the check. Many foreign-made bicycles, however, do not have serial numbers.

In addition to the manufacturer's serial number, you can add some personal identification of your own—such as your Social Security number or your telephone number—to the bicycle. A metal-stamping kit can make this a permanent part of your bicycle. These kits are often available on loan at police departments and at some bicycle dealerships. Or they can be purchased in case you want one for marking not only bicycles, but other valuables as well.

Do not stamp numbers on high-stress locations or thin metal areas of the bicycle frame. The stamping can weaken the metal at these points and could contribute to a broken frame. One commonly used location is under the crank hanger; although this area is subject to high stress, it is suitably strengthened by the thickness of the metal.

In addition to serial numbers, manufacturers are required to mark each major component with a code. These marks, however, are of little help in identifying a bicycle, because the component for an entire group of bicycles may bear the same mark to facilitate procedures if the manufacturer must recall a bicycle for adjustment.

Another way to give your bicycle a personal label is to write a little note and insert it in one or both tires. On this slip of paper write your name, address and phone number, and the request, "If this bicycle is brought to you by any other person, please contact me." The likelihood of catching a thief red-handed, removing a tire and proving that the bicycle is yours may be small. But there is a good possibility that the bicycle may find its way into a shop for tire repair or replacement, and the person who took it may not think of examining the insides of tires.

Stolen bicycles are usually difficult to trace because there is no universal system of registration. Most places do not require registration of any

The bicycle left alone and not protected by lock and key is an easy mark for thieves. BICYCLE MANUFACTURERS ASSOCIATION OF AMERICA, INC., PHOTO.

Police programs for registering bicycles are an aid in helping locate stolen property. U. S. DEPARTMENT OF TRANSPORTATION PHOTO, JAMES CARROLL.

kind; therefore, local police departments or vehicle registration departments seldom have bicycle serial numbers on file. Statewide registration systems could help in the tracing of stolen bicycles. This was one of the conclusions following a study of the place of the bicycle in the community life of Davis, California. "Bicycle registration," said the study, "should be mandatory statewide." The next best alternative, according to this study, would be regional systems of registration. Even that would help trace stolen bicycles beyond the jurisdiction of the local police.

In Naples, Florida, where owners lose an estimated $30,000 worth of bicycles annually, the police department, cooperating with the Optimists Club, helped curb losses through a volunteer bicycle registration plan. The fraternal organization purchased a metal-marking kit so that special identification numbers could be stamped on bicycles, and also paid the printing cost of registration cards. Then both adults and younger riders took their bicycles to one of a number of locations at an announced time. Police reported that the plan did help them trace stolen bicycles and return them to their owners.

Bicycle dealers sometimes retain records of sales, including the serial numbers of bikes sold and who bought them, but no owner should fail to keep the record personally. The chances are that the store will not be able to help you prove ownership.

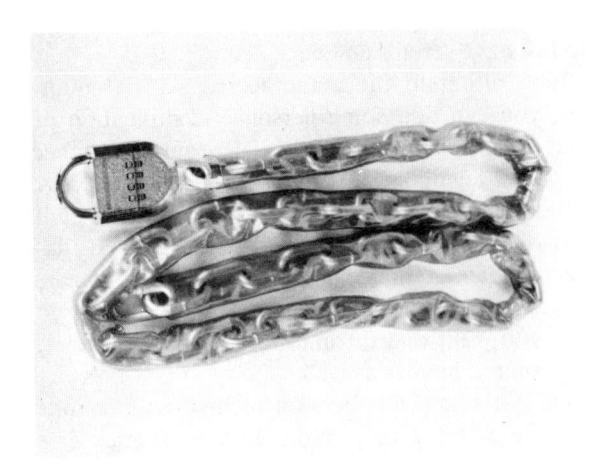

Rugged bicycle lock with six-foot-long, $9/32''$ diameter, case-hardened steel chain with plastic cover. PRESTO LOCK COMPANY.

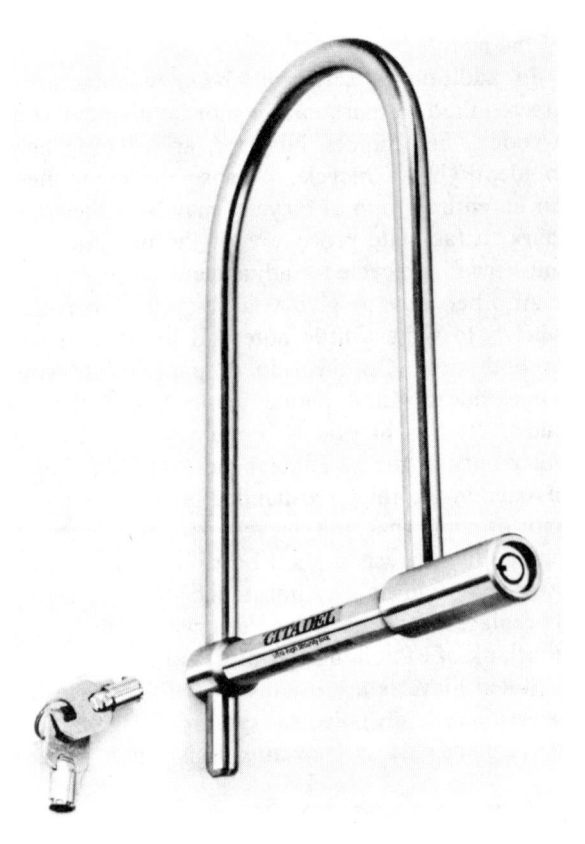

LOCKS AND CHAINS

Many an owner has left a bicycle unprotected outside a shop, school or home on the theory that nobody was going to take it because he would only be gone a minute. That's all it takes. The biggest single protection is to lock the bicycle as securely as you can, even if you expect to be back in a flash. The lock and chain, although they add weight, are worth carrying. The usual practice is to coil the cable or chain and carry it and the lock beneath the saddle.

You will find a wide choice of locks. Some of the cheap ones are only slightly better than nothing as protection from the professional thief, equipped with a pair of bolt cutters. But the lock, properly used, is going to discourage at least those who might take the bike on impulse. The

Citadel bicycle lock frustrates bicycle thieves. ACRO-FAB INDUSTRIES, INC.

THE BIKE STEALERS

Riders make it more difficult for thieves by locking both wheels of the bike to a stationary object. BICYCLE MANUFACTURERS ASSOCIATION OF AMERICA, INC., PHOTO.

more you can slow a thief down, the more you discourage him.

Among the strongest locks available today, and the most expensive, are the large U-shaped locks that are used without chains. The Citadel, for example, a very popular bicycle lock, is made of ½-inch-thick hardened steel alloy that makes a thief's work extremely difficult whether he is using a bolt cutter, a hacksaw or a hammer.

The next best choice is a heavy-duty key lock with chain or cable. Some chains and cables are covered or plastic-coated to prevent scratching bike surfaces. I prefer a key-operated lock over a combination lock, but a cheap lock of either kind is easily opened.

Bicycles with quick-release wheels are especially vulnerable to thieves, partly because they are higher-value machines and partly because there may be at least one wheel left unlocked. The unprotected wheel can be removed in seconds, leaving the owner a kind of unicycle. There are two things you can do. One is to carry a chain or cable long enough to extend through both wheels *and* the frame. The other is to remove the front wheel each time you park and lock it to the frame and back wheel, which is the recommended procedure for locks such as the Citadel.

The bicycle must be locked to something that secures it. Lampposts and permanently installed bike racks are commonly used.

There is a trend toward providing better security services to cyclists who must park their bikes outside office buildings and apartment houses. Some places now provide coin-operated lockers for bicycles. There is also a rising interest in providing racks that give special security against bolt cutters. Some have built-in locking devices, others are designed to permit the owner to use his or her own lock.

HELPFUL TIPS

1. Lock your bicycle to a stationary anchor, whether a tree, lamppost or iron fence.

2. Use the best lock you can afford. The lock should be a heavy-duty case-hardened one with a shackle of at least ⅜ inch in diameter.

3. The best place to leave your locked bicycle is where people will be around it frequently. Bicycles left in hidden locations give thieves freedom to work.

4. Never leave a bicycle unlocked, even for a couple of minutes.

5. Put your bicycle inside at night. Leaving it outdoors anywhere at night is an invitation to thieves.

6. If your bicycle has quick-release hubs, either run the chain and lock through both wheels and the frame or take the front wheel with you. A thief is likely to pass up a bike with only one wheel.

7. Keep a record of your bicycle serial number.

8. Register your bicycle, by name, number and manufacturer, with your local police, if the police department keeps such information on file.

9. Keep a color photograph of your bicycle to help police find it.

10. List your bicycle color, model, make and serial number on any insurance policy that covers personal property.

19.

BICYCLE MAINTENANCE

Most bicycle owners could and should do more of their own maintenance. For one reason, the more you know about the condition of your machine and keeping it in first-rate running order, the longer it will last and the better it is going to perform. Modern multi-geared bicycles need a certain amount of fine tuning from time to time, and as the rider comes to understand his bicycle, he senses changes in it and knows when adjustments are in order.

This ability is especially valuable if you use your bicycle for touring. Even in the city there is no guarantee that you are going to find competent bicycle mechanics when needed. The supply of mechanics has lagged well behind the overall boom in the bicycle industry. Furthermore, labor rates have soared and no hired mechanic has as much interest in your bicycle as you do.

Schwinn stores generally have reliable service departments. Your best tactic, no matter where you live, is to ask experienced bicyclists to recommend bicycle repair shops. Even if you do find a good shop, however, doing the job yourself will save you time and money. A bicycle in a shop for repairs may be out of service for a considerable period, until the mechanics get around to it.

For these reasons, the bicycle owner should study the bicycle, acquire essential tools, and learn as much as possible about replacing parts or adjusting them. Many bicycle repairs are less complicated than they seem at first, but patience is important. Repair work takes time, and the less accomplished you are the more time you will need.

Bicycle clubs sometimes include maintenance and repair sessions in their calendar of club activities. Maintenance clinics are often scheduled for spring, when members want their machines in top condition for the new season.

The tools you need will depend on how deeply you intend to get into the business of repairing bicycles. For minimal repairs and the usual periodic maintenance, the roadside tool kit you carry on your bicycle will do most jobs. Anyone who has worked long with bicycles, however, will soon accumulate other tools. For repairs done at home, I would add the following items. First, equip yourself with a supply of lubricants, both a small can of lightweight oil and a spray can of some special product such as LPD-9 to get at the hard-to-reach places. Add an adjustable wrench and a universal bicycle wrench. A screwdriver or two and a pair of pliers, preferably with side cutting edges, will prove useful. Also include a rivet extractor for chain cleaning and repairs and a spoke wrench if you want to attempt the delicate and demanding business of replacing spokes and truing wheels. Other special tools will be needed for more complex tasks. You may want a freewheel remover, which will enable you to work on the hub and freewheel or change sprockets. There are also special tools for working on the bottom bracket. Take care to see that tools pur-

Cyclists should learn the location of the bicycle shop in their vicinity with the greatest number of skilled mechanics and the best supplies of equipment. BICYCLE MANUFACTURERS ASSOCIATION OF AMERICA, INC., PHOTO.

BICYCLE MAINTENANCE

chased fit your bicycle's components. Metric tools are needed for many bicycles made today, especially those of foreign manufacture. Some of the household tools you already have can be used for bicycle repairs. These include a small hammer with a plastic or rubber head, small metric socket wrenches and needle-nose pliers.

PEDAL CARE

Pedals that are wobbly or do not work smoothly must be adjusted or replaced. There is not much that can be accomplished by trying to repair the less expensive pedals, although rubber blocks can be replaced when they are badly worn if the pedal is otherwise in good condition.

Selecting pedals to fit your bicycle may be more difficult than you would think. Manufacturers have not standardized thread measurements. Unless the pedal screws into the end of the crank easily and smoothly by hand for several turns, it is probably the wrong fit. Remember that pedals on opposite sides of the bicycle have threads turning in opposite directions, left-hand threads on the left side, right-hand threads on the right side. When replacing a pedal it is a good idea to apply a light coat of grease to the threads. Then, if the threads are clean and the pedal fits properly, you can get it started easily by hand and later remove it with reasonable ease.

TIRE REPAIRS

Anyone who rides a bicycle can expect flat tires. Tire repairs can be—and often are—handled on the roadside with minimum delay. Be certain before starting on a trip that you have included a tire repair kit for the kind of tires you use, either clincher-type or tubular (sew-up) tires. Also carry an extra tube for clincher tires, and an extra tire if you use sew-ups.

The clincher tires—more common, less costly and easier to repair than tubulars—have a wire embedded along the inside edge to help hold the tire secure against the rim. Both kinds of tires are fitted with inner tubes. The two types are made to fit different rim designs. If you want to ride on clincher tires part of the time, and tubular tires on special occasions, you can keep two complete sets of wheels ready to go. With quick-release wheels you can change from one kind to the other instantly.

One essential to long tire life is proper inflation. The under-inflated tire can develop weakened walls, a pinched tube or a rim cut in the sidewall, any of which can puncture the tube and perhaps necessitate replacing the tire. If you always inflate the tires with a hand pump, the chances are that you will not over-inflate dangerously. Serious bicyclists steer clear of service station air pumps. They also learn to rely on the "feel" of the tire to tell if it needs air.

Regular inspection of tires is important, especially if you are riding far from home. Before starting on a tour, always consider the condition of your tires. If the tread is thin, the chances of picking up bits of glass or other materials that cause punctures are greater. Inspect tires for foreign materials caught in the treads or along the rim.

CLINCHER TIRE REPAIR

For repairing clincher tires you will need, in addition to your patch kit, a pair of tire levers, which you can buy at low cost from your bicycle shop. These levers have dull edges that are less likely to damage tires and tubes than are sharp-edged screwdrivers or other tools.

If your tire is losing air slowly, the trouble might be with the valve. You may correct this by simply tightening or replacing the valve core. Cover the open end of the valve with liquid and see if escaping air blows bubbles.

For punctures where you will have to patch the tube, you may or may not be able to locate the hole easily. After partly inflating the tube, listen for escaping air. If this doesn't work, submerge the tire in water and locate the hole by the air bubbles.

The actual patching is handled in the same manner as described below for tubulars. When you are ready to replace the patched tube, inflate it slightly for easier handling. Take care to get the valve straight in its rim hole, then force the

A good hand pump with a press-on head makes it easy to keep tires fully inflated. PHOTO BY THE AUTHOR.

Riders should make frequent checks of air pressure and should keep tires inflated to recommended levels for easier riding and better tire maintenance. PHOTO BY THE AUTHOR.

tire back onto the rim, a job you should be able to do with your hands alone. Work carefully, because even without using tire tools there is the possibility of pinching the tube between tire and rim and puncturing it again.

Repairing tubulars is somewhat more complicated than working with clincher tires, because tubulars are sewn shut after the tube is in place. The thin tube is protected from the stitching by a protective cloth inside the tire; the tire is shielded from the rim and the spoke heads by a rim strip, glued in place.

If a tubular develops a leak, here are the major steps in fixing it. Buy a repair kit especially made for tubulars. Regular tire-repair kits will not have the very thin patches needed for tubulars, or the waxed thread and needle for sewing them.

First, find the leak and mark the spot with chalk. Next, peel back the rim strip, which is a strip of cloth glued or sewn in place to protect the tire stitching and keep the tire in place on the rim. Peel the strip back several inches on either side of the puncture to get at the tire stitching.

The next task is to open the tire by cutting the stitches for a few inches on either side of the puncture. A slip at this point can make a second hole in the tire or tube. Fold the tire in the middle of the stitching and work the edge of a very sharp knife or safety razor blade under the stitches to cut them one at a time. Remove the cut threads. Now you can pull a portion of the tube out of the casing so you can get at it for patching.

The tube must be dry and clean. Using sandpaper, roughen the thin tube in the area around the puncture and wipe off any crumbs of rubber. Next, coat the area with the cement from the repair kit. Let this set. Be sure to avoid letting oil from your fingers adhere to the rubber or to the inner surface of the patch: it will prevent an airtight seal. Carefully strip the backing from the patch and position it over the puncture, then press it firmly to obtain a secure contact. If the casing has an obvious puncture you may also have to apply a small patch on the inside. This will work for a road repair, but the tire will probably never again give you satisfactory service for any considerable distance.

Once the tube is patched you are ready to replace the protective cloth over it and sew it back in place inside the tire, using waxed thread and needle, and perhaps also a thimble. What you must do is use the same holes for these new stitches that were made for the original stitches, and the holes on either side of the casing have to be lined up to match. Starting a few stitches behind the first ones that were cut, sew the casing and pull the thread snug enough to hold the edges together but not so tight that it causes the casing to buckle or overlap. Your stitches should hold the thread ends, so no knots are needed. Take care, while stitching the tubular, not to puncture the tube again.

To secure the rim strip, apply a thin coat of rubber cement to both it and the tire. Let this dry briefly, then secure the rim strip to the tire smoothly.

As your sew-ups age they are going to lose air increasingly, because the thin rubber from which they are made is somewhat porous and weakens. If one leaks too fast and you cannot find the source of the trouble, you may have to replace it. Some bicyclists, after an initial try, quickly give up efforts to repair these tires and resign themselves to buying replacements as needed.

When you are ready to remount the tire on the rim, apply a coat of rim cement or use rim tape cemented on both sides. Begin by inserting the valve, and be certain that it is straight in the hole. Using both hands, and only hands, begin working the tire back into place. The pressure of your thumbs should enable you to get the last section of the tire back on the rim. Then inflate it partly to hold it firmly in place. After the rim cement is dry you can bring the air pressure up to the recommended level.

Frequent inspection of tubulars is important. Remove any foreign materials from the tire. Modern tubulars, given good care, can be almost as trouble-free as clinchers on trips.

DERAILLEUR PROBLEMS

If the derailleur is not working quietly and smoothly, the answer may be as simple as adjusting the screws that control it. Turn to your operator's manual and study the information on the derailleur system used on your bicycle. Also study the derailleur itself. There are gear-chain stops for both the high and low gears. These keep the chain from traveling too far to the right or left when changing gears. These adjustment screws are found in various places on the derailleur, depending on which system your bicycle uses. You can tell the low-gear stop and the high-gear stop apart by hanging the bike up or turning it over and shifting gears while turning the crank. The chain stops prevent the chain from moving farther than it should. Traveling in foul weather or taking a fall can throw the derailleur out of adjustment. Riders of average experience often find the derailleur system confusing. If this is your situation, you may want to take the derailleur repair job to a good bicycle shop. But if you are a long way from home, you will find comfort in the knowledge that you have learned to handle the easier adjustments yourself.

CHAIN CARE

The chain that becomes dirty—sometimes you can actually hear the grit grinding in it—should be cleaned. It is good practice to clean the chain anyhow every few months if you ride regularly. The best way to clean a chain is to remove it—a process that is less complicated than it might seem to be. Bicycles without derailleurs normally have chains equipped with connector links that can be opened without a special tool. Derailleur-equipped bicycles, however, have no such special links, and consequently you need a chain rivet extractor. This inexpensive device, available at any bicycle shop, is small enough to carry conveniently in your tool kit, along with a few spare chain links, for those occasions when roadside repairs are needed.

You can remove the chain from a ten-speed more easily if it is on the smallest cog. This gives you slack to work the chain-link tool. Remove any link by using the tool to drive the rivet part way out. Before pulling the chain out from the front, take a look at how it rides through the derailleurs so you can return it to its proper location with minimum trouble.

To clean the chain, coil it loosely in a flat pan with enough kerosene to cover it. Let it soak for

Obtain a spray can of special lubricant from your bicycle shop and use it sparingly but frequently to keep the chain clean and working smoothly. PHOTO BY THE AUTHOR.

half an hour or so, or clean it with an old toothbrush. Although some cyclists wipe the chain dry with a cloth, it's better to hang it to dry in an area free of dust.

Lubricating the chain too heavily attracts dirt and grit, which cause excess wear. Use a very light oil or a lubricant such as LPS-3. Bicycle shops stock lubricants especially recommended for chains. After lubricating the chain, wipe it off lightly with a clean cloth. When the chain is clean, run it back through the derailleurs and use the chain-vise capability of the rivet extractor to replace the link.

INSPECT THE FRAME

As part of your regular inspection, especially prior to starting a long ride, take time to check the bicycle frame. Frame weaknesses with the potential of developing into breaks could bring an abrupt interruption to your tour and might also put you in a hazardous situation. Breaks are possible even with frames built of the high-quality, lightweight, flexible double-butted tubing.

Check the joints where tubing comes together and look especially for tiny cracks that could grow. Lugs and seams throughout should fit snugly. Look on all sides of the tubing for

BICYCLE MAINTENANCE

In the course of regular monthly bicycle maintenance, check to see that nuts and bolts are tight. BICYCLE MANUFACTURERS ASSOCIATION OF AMERICA, INC., PHOTO.

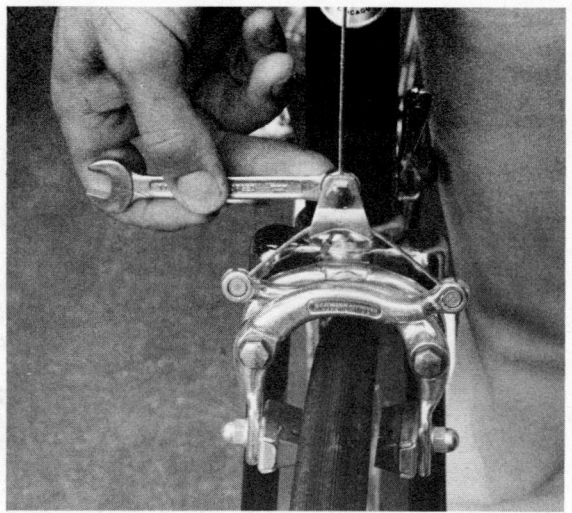

Caliper brake shoes should be checked periodically to make sure that they are not worn excessively and that they are no more than ¼ inch from the wheel rims. Cable lengths can be easily adjusted with the aid of an open-end wrench and a pair of pliers to put proper tension on the cable. PHOTO BY THE AUTHOR.

breaks. Also check the forks to see that there are no cracks in any part of them. This is not a problem frequently met and most of the time when it does happen the trouble is not detected in advance.

If there is a crack, even a very little one, you should have the machine inspected by a competent bicycle mechanic. A substantial shock on the road might enlarge the fracture, or even break the frame. The mechanic can tell you whether or not damage to the frame is repairable. If it cannot be fixed, you may have to change bicycles.

GIVE YOUR BIKE REGULAR CHECKUPS

One way to be certain you remember to check your bicycle regularly is to inspect it on a certain day each month, perhaps the first day of the month. Go over the machine and check off the items needing monthly inspection. If the bicycle gets heavy use, you may check these points more frequently. If it is not being used regularly, as might be the case in winter, you can safely put off the check until you resume riding.

Here are parts that should be included in any monthly checkup and lubrication.

BRAKE AND DERAILLEUR CABLES. See that cables are not worn or frayed and that levers are in good working order. Give the cables a few drops of lightweight oil, applying it where they go into the tubing. Whenever cables are replaced, they should be greased before being put into the housings. Taking cables off to lubricate them is not very complicated, but you may want to take your bicycle to the bike shop for the cable work if more is involved than the regular monthly checkup and minor lubrication.

BRAKE SHOES. Check the pads that press against the rims to see that the brake shoes contact the rim properly, are not heavily worn and are set within ⅛ of an inch from the rim. Keep oil and grease off the pads.

PEDALS. Check them to see that they are tight, that they turn freely and that parts are not seriously worn. Rattrap pedals will not need lubrication. If your bicycle is equipped with American-style pedals, treat them to a few drops of medium-weight oil at each end.

FRONT HUB, REAR HUB. Lubricate lightly if there is a provision on it for grease or oil.

Handlebars should be kept straight and tight. Stems for handlebars come in a wide variety; the length should be selected to match the rider's arm length. There should never be less than 2½ inches of stem down inside the fork tube. Some stems have this minimum insertion distance marked. BICYCLE MANUFACTURERS ASSOCIATION OF AMERICA, INC., PHOTO.

Seat should be adjusted to a line level with the top of the handlebar post, with the front of the seat slightly higher than the back. Proper height for the seat is 1.09 times the rider's leg length from crotch to ground. PHOTO BY THE AUTHOR.

DERAILLEURS. Using lightweight oil, lubricate lightly the pivot points of both front and rear derailleurs. Also give the gear-shift levers a few drops of oil. Too much oil gives dirt a place to accumulate.

FREEWHEELS. Use a few drops of lightweight oil on the freewheel, taking care not to overdo the oiling.

HANDLEBARS. Does the handlebar stem face forward squarely? Is it tight? Do the handlebar grips or the tape need replacing? Anytime you adjust handlebars, remember that there should always be at least 2½ inches of the stem inside the head tube.

WHEELS. Lift the end of the bike or turn it over, then spin the wheels to see if they wobble. They should run straight and true. If they are out of line, the problem may lie in a bent rim or loose spokes. This is a good time to check spokes to see that all are in good condition and tight.

SADDLE. Saddles can work loose and should be checked periodically to see that they are positioned properly and nuts are tight.

LIGHTS AND REFLECTORS. If you have not used the lights recently, batteries may be worn out or connections may be corroded. Reflectors should still be secure in their proper locations and set at correct angles, generally the position of the reflectors when the new bike came from the store.

TIRES. Check for cuts, breaks, worn tread and valves out of their straight forward position, as well as proper inflation.

CLEAN IT UP. Using a soft cloth, go over the bicycle and clean dust and dirt from all the surfaces to give it that new-bike shine. If the saddle needs washing, use warm water and soap. You are likely to take greater pride in a bicycle that looks well kept.

NOTES